PUBLISHER'S NOTE

V&S Publishers has carved a significant niche in the publishing industry over the last decade, having successfully published more than 1000 titles across 9 languages spanning over 50 subject categories. Being known for the quality of content, we have built a reputation of excellence and reliability. We have consistently delivered **"Value & Substance"** to our readers, through a wide range of titles across a variety of genres covering school books, fiction and non-fiction that caters to different people from every section of the society.

The **Olympiad Guidebooks for classes 1-10** across all subjects, launched almost a decade ago, under the **GEN X Imprint**, became a go-to-source for the school students in no time, owing to their invaluable and substantive content written in a guidebook pattern,.

Having successfully sold a million copies of the same and in response to demand by both students as well as shopkeepers nationwide; we now present before you our newly launched **Olympiad Workbook Series**, designed for **classes 1-10 across 4 subjects**.

The workbooks are meticulously curated by a team of experienced educators, researchers and subject matter experts, edited by professionals and peer reviewed by teachers. The team has poured its efforts and expertise into creating a crisp and concise workbook which will help and guide the students to the path of success in Olympiad exams. The **MCQs** identified will not only help in scoring top marks in Olympiads but also inculcate a sense of deeper understanding of the subject, by way of solving **HOTS** and referring to complete solutions at the end of the book.

Here we present our new release– **OLYMPIAD WORKBOOK (NSO) CLASS–4** having following features:

- ☞ Based on the latest syllabi
- ☞ MCQs with comprehensive coverage of topics
- ☞ HOTS Questions liberally included
- ☞ A dedicated chapter on logical reasoning
- ☞ Model test paper for thorough practice
- ☞ Sample OMR sheet for real time simulation

We have made sure through our best efforts, that this workbook strictly follows the latest syllabi and patterns of the Olympiad Examination.

As **V&S Publishers** continuously strive to enhance the readability and maintain the credibility of our academic publications, we seek the support of our valuable readers in influencing and enriching the lives of future generations of students.

P.S. While every care has been taken to ensure the correctness of the content, if you come across any error, howsoever minor, do not hesitate to discuss with teachers while pointing that out to us in no uncertain terms.

We wish you all the best for your exams!

DISTINCTIVE FEATURES

01 Learning Objectives

They list the whole chapter as subtopics, helping the teachers to guide children in a step-by-step manner.

02 Multiple Choice Questions

MCQs act as an excellent learning aid, helping you to understand and work on your mistakes.

03 HOTS (Achievers Section)

The High Order Thinking Questions aim to help the student to solve Application-based questions and gain practical understanding of the subject.

04 Model Test Paper

Model test paper are provided at the end of each book, which help the student to test the knowledge which they have gained after thorough reading of all chapters.

05 Answer Key

Detailed Answer Key along with explanations aid the pupil to indentify, understand the mistakes they make during the course of Olympiad preparation.

CONTENTS

PLANT LIFE

1

LEARNING OBJECTIVES

➤ Importance of plants in the environment
➤ Different parts of plants and their function
➤ The process of photosynthesis

MULTIPLE CHOICE QUESTIONS

Direction: Select the correct option for each of the following questions.

1. Photosynthesis is the process by which plants convert _____________.
   - (A) Sugar and sunlight into oxygen
   - (B) Sugar and oxygen into carbon dioxide and energy
   - (C) Carbon dioxide and water into sugar and oxygen
   - (D) Sunlight into oxygen

2. The loss of water through the leaves of a plant is called _____________.
   - (A) Inspiration
   - (B) Expiration
   - (C) Transpiration
   - (D) Photosynthesis

3. The stomata are the pores in the leaf. Their function is to take in _____________.
   - (A) Carbon dioxide for photosynthesis
   - (B) Oxygen for photosynthesis
   - (C) Carbon dioxide for respiration
   - (D) Oxygen for respiration

4. During what time of the day does the process shown in the picture take place in plants?

   - (A) 11 am
   - (B) 6 am
   - (C) 2 pm
   - (D) All the time

5. Study the figure given here and identify the gases X and Y.

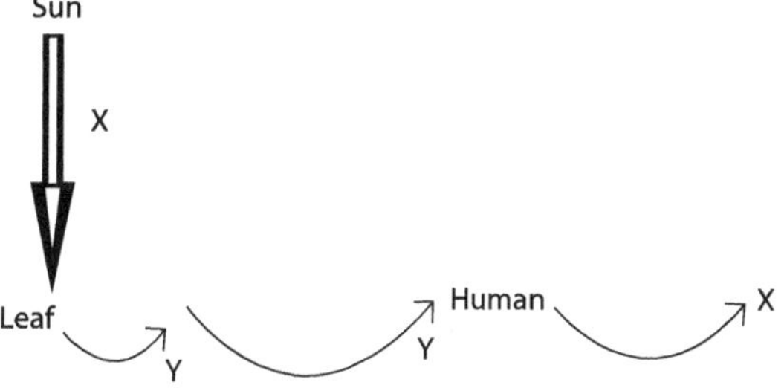

   - (A) X - Oxygen, Y - Carbon dioxide
   - (B) X - Hydrogen, Y - Nitrogen
   - (C) X - Carbon dioxide, Y - Oxygen
   - (D) X - Nitrogen, Y - Hydrogen

6. What does etiolation mean?
   (A) Leaves become yellow due to the reduced light.
   (B) Leaves become yellow due to the breaking down of the chlorophyll.
   (C) Leaves become brown due to the breaking down of the chlorophyll.
   (D) In the absence of light or greatly reduced light, leaves become yellow due to the breaking down of the chlorophyll.

7. Mushroom gets its food from __________.
   (A) The water we pour near it
   (B) Dead and decaying plants
   (C) Photosynthesis
   (D) Eating small insects that come near it

8. Plants store extra food in the form of __________.
   (A) Carbon dioxide   (B) Starch
   (C) Oxygen   (D) Chlorophyll

9. In the carrot, food is stored in the __________.
   (A) Stem   (B) Leaves
   (C) Flowers   (D) Roots

10. Water is taken from the surroundings into the plant through the __________.
    (A) Leaves   (B) Roots
    (C) Stems   (D) Flower

11. An example of a fruit containing seeds that is edible to humans is a __________.
    (A)    (B) 
    (C)    (D)

12. The main purpose of flowers is to provide __________.
    (A) Support   (B) Food
    (C) Water   (D) Seed

13. Leaves provide the surface area necessary for __________.
    (A) Absorption of sunlight, which begins the process of photosynthesis.
    (B) Absorption of carbon dioxide, which begins the process of photosynthesis.
    (C) Absorption of water, which begins the process of photosynthesis.
    (D) None of these

14. Which of the following statements is/are true?
    i.   Plants are living organisms.
    ii. All organisms including plants are composed of cells, grow, reproduce, and respond to various kinds of stimuli like temperature.
    iii. Sea anemone is a plant.
    iv. Plants have the ability to manufacture food, which distinguishes them from other living organisms.
    (A) i and ii   (B) ii and iii
    (C) i, ii and iv   (D) i and iii

15. Which of the following structures of plant exchange gases?
    (A) Flower   (B) Leaves
    (C) Buds   (D) Fruits

16. Which of the following instruments is used to examine the cells of a leaf?
    (A) Telescope
    (B) Magnifying glass
    (C) Camera
    (D) Microscope

17. The tiny pores present on the leaves of plants are called __________.
    (A) Chlorophyll
    (B) Cells
    (C) Grains
    (D) Stomata

18. Spines in cacti are __________.
    (A) Modified stems
    (B) Modified roots
    (C) Modifies leaves
    (D) Can be any of the above

19. They grow underground, but while we might think of them as roots, they are actually a specified part of the plant's stem.

(A) Carrots   (B) Beets
(C) Potatoes   (D) Radishes

20. Asparagus is a __________.
 (A) Root   (B) Stem
 (C) Leaf   (D) Flower

21. The secondary stems grow out from the main stem, and these stems have ______.
 (A) Thistles   (B) Flowers
 (C) Leaves   (D) Stems

22. Roots and stems carry __________.
 (A) Sunlight and sugar
 (B) Nutrients and water
 (C) Carbon dioxide and sugar
 (D) Oxygen and nutrients

23. One day when Ananya was holding her sunflower plant, the stem of the plant accidentally broke. Her plant died two days later. Why?
 i. The plant could not transport food made by the leaves to the rest of the plant.
 ii. The plant lost too much water through the break in the stem.
 iii. The plant could not transport water from the roots to the leaves.
 (A) i   (B) iii
 (C) i and iii   (D) ii and iii

24. This plant is found in Australia. It has very few leaves. Local people put a thin pipe into the trunk of this tree to drink water. This tree is __________.
 (A) Spinifex   (B) Oak
 (C) Cactus   (D) Bamboo

25. Look at the following picture of leaves and identify the plant or tree name ______.

(A) Gulmohar   (B) Pine
(C) Neem   (D) Mango

26. There are four plants __________.

Coconut tree	Cactus
Mushroom	Mimosa

 Among those four, mushroom should be categorized differently because ________.
 i. The mushroom feeds on decaying things while the rest do not.
 ii. The mushroom is a plant while the rest are not.
 iii. The mushroom is a fungus while the rest are not.
 iv. The mushroom cannot make its own food while the rest can.
 (A) i and ii
 (B) i, iii, and iv
 (C) ii and iii
 (D) Only iv

27. Anish and his friends set up an experiment as shown below:

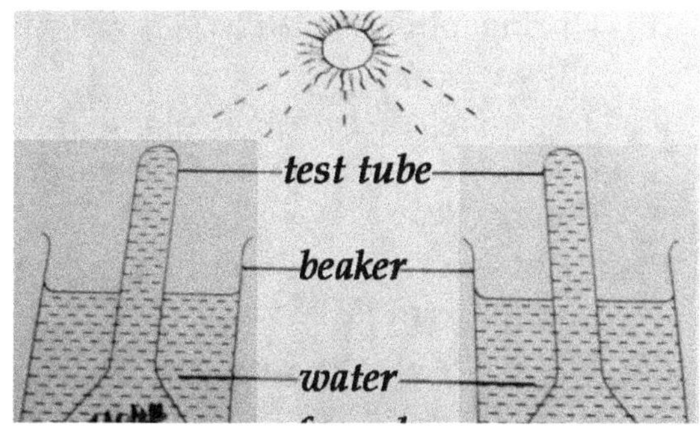

Hydrilla

 They left the set-up in bright sunlight for four hours. What would they observe at the end of the four hours?
 (A) A gas would collect in test tube A and B
 (B) A gas would collect in the entire set-up
 (C) A gas would collect in test tube A but not in test tube B
 (D) Nothing will happen

28. Saumya performed an activity as follows: She took a plant with many leaves. Then she covered a healthy leaf of that plant completely with some black paper and left the plant in the open for three days. Finally she performed starch test on both the leaves.

What would happen?
(A) Covered leaves would turn blue
(B) Uncovered leaves would turn blue
(C) Nothing will happen
(D) All leaves, covered and uncovered, would turn blue

29. Which part of a sugarcane plant contains food?
(A) Fruit   (B) Stem
(C) Root   (D) Leaf

30. Which of the following processes increases the amount of carbon dioxide in the air?
(A) Perspiration
(B) Photosynthesis
(C) Respiration
(D) Transpiration

HOTS (ACHIEVERS SECTION)

31. The leaf is that part of a plant, which is responsible for the process of photosynthesis.
(A) Leaves help plants by balancing the water in the plant.
(B) During photosynthesis, leaves give out oxygen.
(C) To make their food, plants need energy from the sun. This work is done by leaves.
P: Point B and C are describing process of photosynthesis.
Q: Point B is describing the process of interchange of gases.
R: Point A and C are describing the process of evaporation of water.
S: All the points are describing the process of photosynthesis.

Now, choose the correct answer from the following options.
(A) P and S   (B) P and Q
(C) R and S   (D) Only P

32. A student measures and records the growth of two flowering plants every other day for 10 days.

According to the diagram, which parameter is being tested?

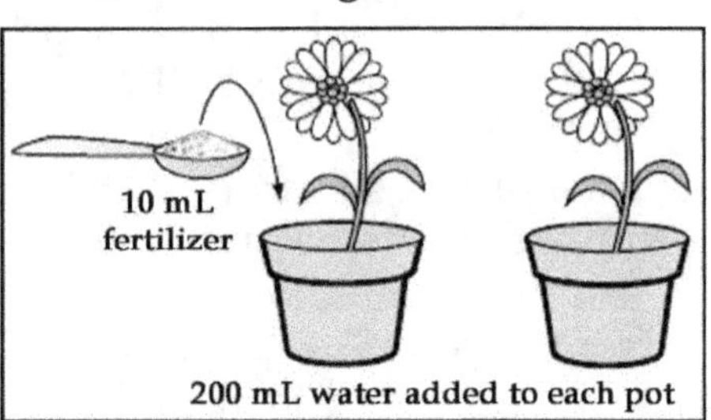

(A) Does fertilizer added to the soil lead to taller flowering plants?
(B) How tall do flowering plants grow?
(C) Do flowering plants grow better when watered with salt water?
(D) How much fertilizer do flowering plants need?

33. Which of the following is not a benefit of plants/trees?
(A) They bind the soil.
(B) They stop soil erosion.
(C) They give out Hydrogen gas.
(D) They provide us fruits and vegetables.

34. Abhi covered a leaf of a potted plant and kept the plant under sunlight

for a few days and then tested it with iodine solution for the presence of starch in it. The colour of the covered leaf did not turn blue-black. What does this indicate?

(A) The black cover absorbed all the starch present in the leaf.

(B) Iodine solution does not work with black covers.

(C) Starch is evaporated from the leaves.

(D) Starch is prepared only in the presence of sunlight.

35. Which of the following plants will be able to carry out photosynthesis?

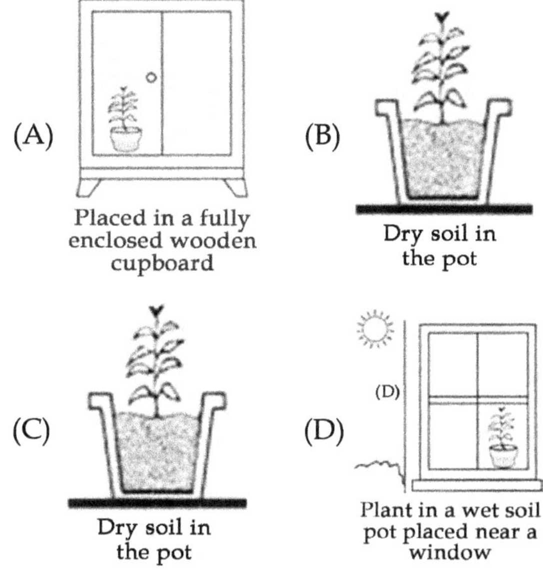

ANIMAL LIFE

➤ Methods of reproduction in animals
➤ How egg-laying animals are different from mammals

MULTIPLE CHOICE QUESTIONS

Direction: Select the correct option for each of the following questions.

1. A student observed that birds sit on their eggs before the eggs hatch into young ones. The reason is to __________.
   (A) Protect the eggs
   (B) Keeps the eggs warm
   (C) Hide the eggs from others
   (D) Make the eggs strong

2. Which is the correct life cycle?
   (A) Baby-teenager-child-adult
   (B) Seed-flower-plant-fruit
   (C) Cocoon-larva-egg-adult
   (D) Egg-caterpillar-pupa-butterfly

3. Which of the following are most similar to tadpoles?
   (A) Frogs   (B) Eggs
   (C) Larvae   (D) Fish

4. The eggs of the fish are called __________.
   (A) Larva   (B) Pupa
   (C) Spawn   (D) Cocoon

5. Animals need to reproduce to __________.
   (A) Maintain their number
   (B) Increase their number
   (C) Maintain the balance of nature
   (D) All of these

6. The larva of the butterfly is called __________.
   (A) Maggot   (B) Nymph
   (C) Cocoon   (D) Caterpillar

7. Which of these animals suckle their young?
   (A) Mammals   (B) Insects
   (C) Reptiles   (D) Cocoons

8. The white part of the egg is called __________.
   (A) Yolk   (B) Albumin
   (C) Egg shell   (D) Caterpillar

9. What does the egg yolk contain that gives energy to the embryo?
   (A) Water   (B) Stored food
   (C) Soil   (D) Sunlight

10. At which stage does the organism cover itself in a cocoon?
    (A) Egg   (B) Larva
    (C) Pupa   (D) Butterfly

11. At the egg stage, energy is obtained from __________.
    (A) The leaves of the plant
    (B) Egg yolk present in the egg
    (C) Killing other insects
    (D) Photosynthesis

12. At the larva stage, energy is obtained from:
    (A) Egg yolk
    (B) Leaves
    (C) Photosynthesis
    (D) Soil
13. Mammals have __________.
    (A) Constant body temperature
    (B) Changing body temperature
    (C) High temperature at night and low temperature during the day
    (D) No temperature

The following diagram represents the life cycle of a frog.

    EGG -------------- TADPOLE -------------- FROG

Answer the following questions (14–17) based on Fig. 3 on page 34.

14. A tadpole resembles __________.
    (A) Frog   (B) Egg
    (C) Fish   (D) Cocoon
15. Which of the following is possessed by the tadpole but not the adult frog?
    (A) Eye   (B) Tail
    (C) Kidney   (D) Lungs
16. A dolphin is __________.
    (A) A mammal
    (B) An egg-laying animal
    (C) A fish
    (D) An egg-laying fish
17. Which of the following is not a part of egg?
    (A) Umbical cord   (B) Yolk
    (C) Shell   (D) Albumin
18. Match the following __________.

a.	Caterpillar	i.	Frog
b.	Nymph	ii.	Housefly
c.	Tadpole	iii.	Butterfly
d.	Maggot	iv.	Cockroach

(A) C-i, D-ii, B-iii, A-iv
(B) B-i, C-ii, D-iii, A-iv
(C) B-i, D-ii, A-iii, C-iv
(D) C-i, D-ii, A-iii, B-iv

19. Which of the following sets consists of only mammals?
    (A) Lion, hen, and human beings
    (B) Lions, goats, and whales
    (C) Tigers, sheep, and crocodiles
    (D) Birds, butterflies, and frogs
20. Nymph – shedding its skin – cockroach is __________.
    (A) Moulting   (B) Reproduction
    (C) Lifecycle   (D) Food chain
21. The beetle has a life cycle similar to the butterfly's. At which stage of the beetle's life cycle does the beetle not feed?

    (A) Egg   (B) Larva
    (C) Pupa   (D) Adult
22. Which of the following animals is a mammal that lays eggs?
    (A) Dolphin   (B) Spiny Anteater
    (C) Duck   (D) Mouse
23 Which of the following animals does not have the life cycle given below?

    (A) Mosquito
    (B) Butterfly
    (C) Mealworm beetle
    (D) Grasshopper

24. In the classification chart below, which animal has been grouped wrongly?

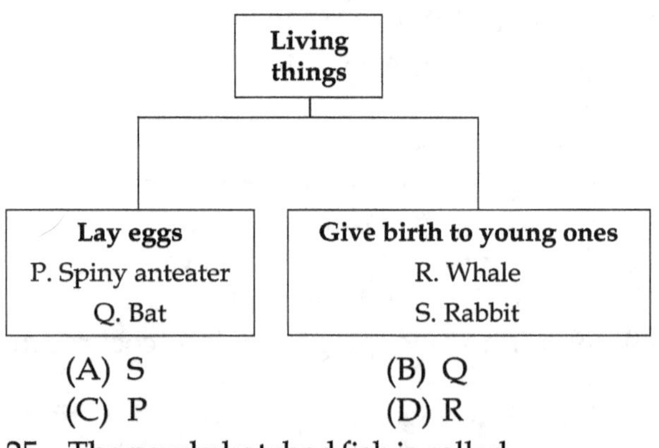

(A) S (B) Q
(C) P (D) R

25. The newly hatched fish is called __________.
(A) Fry (B) Larvae
(C) Nymphs (D) Pupa

26. Which of the following sets of animals represents a group of animals?
(A) Birds, butterfly, and frog
(B) Lion, goat, and whale
(C) Lion, hen, and human beings
(D) Tiger, sheep, and crocodile

27. Which of the following are gnawing animals?

i. Beaver ii. Rat
iii. Squirrel iv. Guinea pig
(A) i and ii (B) i and iii
(C) iii and iv (D) i, ii, iii, and iv

28. Birds build nests __________.
(A) In hedges and bushes
(B) In the hollow of trees
(C) In the dark, wet places
(D) On the branches of tall trees

29. Look at the picture below __________.

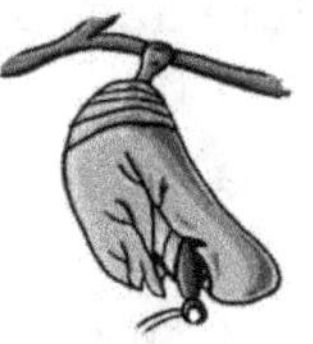

After some time, a __________ will come out of the case shown above.
(A) Cockroach (B) Nymph
(C) Butterfly (D) Caterpillar

30. Which of the following animals has young ones that look similar to the parents?
(A) Frog (B) Butterfly
(C) Lions (D) Mosquito

HOTS (ACHIEVERS SECTION)

31. When comparing fossil A to fossil B, which is most likely correct?

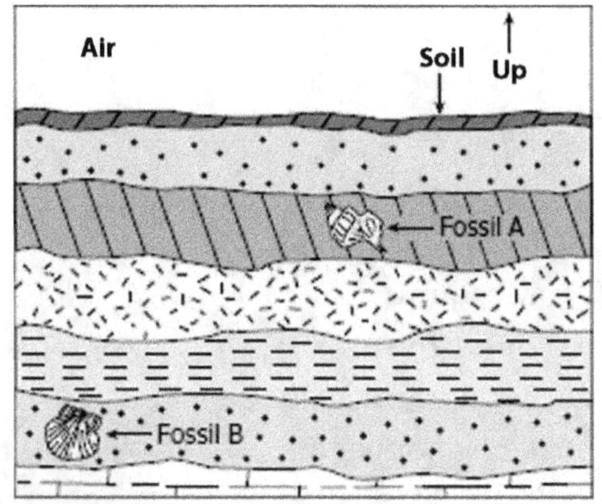

(A) Fossil B is older
(B) Fossil B is larger
(C) Only fossil B is metamorphic
(D) Only fossil B was once an organism

32. Ankita read that woodlice are usually found under piles of damp rotting leaves. She suggested four possible explanations for this behaviour.
i. Woodlice need rotting leaves.
ii. Woodlice find their food there.
iii. Woodlice need dark conditions.
iv. Woodlice need a damp environment.

OLYMPIAD WORKBOOK (NSO) CLASS—4

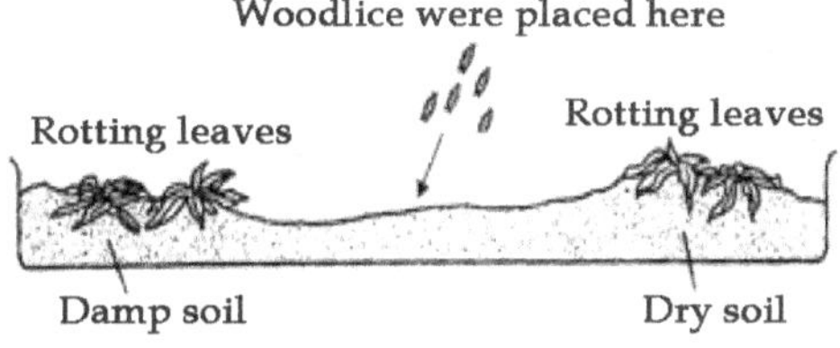

The above diagram shows the experiment which Sarika had conducted. Which above explanation regarding the behaviour of the woodlice was tested by Sarika?

(A) 1   (B) 2

(C) 3   (D) 4

33. Read the list of the animals given below and answer the following question.

Fox, Frog, Mouse, Elephant, Lizard, Duck, Camel, Crow, Pig, Parrot, Buffalo, Zebra

Which of the animals given in the list lay eggs?

(A) Frog, Lizard, Duck, Crow, Parrot

(B) Fox, Frog, Duck, Crow, Parrot

(D) Zebra, Elephant, Mouse, Parrot, Fox

(D) Camel, Mouse, Buffalo, Crow, Pig

34. Which of the following stages can be placed at? in the given life cycle?

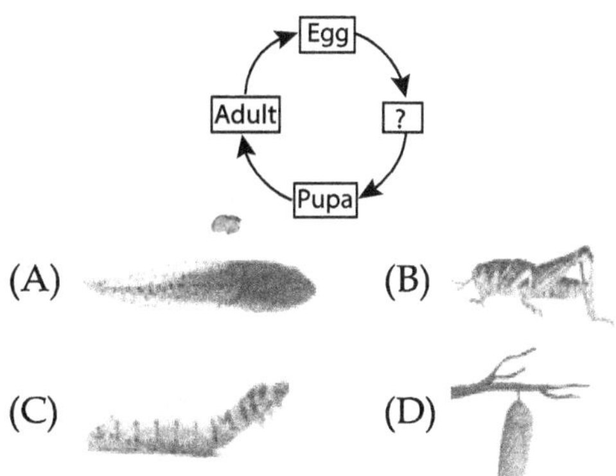

(A)   (B)

(C)   (D)

35. Ten male animals each of type X and Y were living together for few months in captivity in a well-defined area (full of greenery). Other types of animals were not present in this area. Then an animal Z was introduced in this area. After few days, their numbers were counted as shown here.

X	Y	Z
10	2	1

What does this indicate?

(A) Z is a carnivore.

(B) Y is a herbivore.

(C) X is a herbivore.

(D) All of these

Darken Your Choice with HB Pencil

	A B C D		A B C D		A B C D		A B C D		A B C D
1.	Ⓐ Ⓑ Ⓒ Ⓓ	8.	Ⓐ Ⓑ Ⓒ Ⓓ	15.	Ⓐ Ⓑ Ⓒ Ⓓ	22	Ⓐ Ⓑ Ⓒ Ⓓ	29.	Ⓐ Ⓑ Ⓒ Ⓓ
2.	Ⓐ Ⓑ Ⓒ Ⓓ	9.	Ⓐ Ⓑ Ⓒ Ⓓ	16.	Ⓐ Ⓑ Ⓒ Ⓓ	23.	Ⓐ Ⓑ Ⓒ Ⓓ	30.	Ⓐ Ⓑ Ⓒ Ⓓ
3.	Ⓐ Ⓑ Ⓒ Ⓓ	10.	Ⓐ Ⓑ Ⓒ Ⓓ	17.	Ⓐ Ⓑ Ⓒ Ⓓ	24.	Ⓐ Ⓑ Ⓒ Ⓓ	31.	Ⓐ Ⓑ Ⓒ Ⓓ
4.	Ⓐ Ⓑ Ⓒ Ⓓ	11.	Ⓐ Ⓑ Ⓒ Ⓓ	18.	Ⓐ Ⓑ Ⓒ Ⓓ	25.	Ⓐ Ⓑ Ⓒ Ⓓ	32.	Ⓐ Ⓑ Ⓒ Ⓓ
5.	Ⓐ Ⓑ Ⓒ Ⓓ	12.	Ⓐ Ⓑ Ⓒ Ⓓ	19.	Ⓐ Ⓑ Ⓒ Ⓓ	26.	Ⓐ Ⓑ Ⓒ Ⓓ	33.	Ⓐ Ⓑ Ⓒ Ⓓ
6.	Ⓐ Ⓑ Ⓒ Ⓓ	13.	Ⓐ Ⓑ Ⓒ Ⓓ	20.	Ⓐ Ⓑ Ⓒ Ⓓ	27.	Ⓐ Ⓑ Ⓒ Ⓓ	34.	Ⓐ Ⓑ Ⓒ Ⓓ
7.	Ⓐ Ⓑ Ⓒ Ⓓ	14.	Ⓐ Ⓑ Ⓒ Ⓓ	21.	Ⓐ Ⓑ Ⓒ Ⓓ	28.	Ⓐ Ⓑ Ⓒ Ⓓ	35.	Ⓐ Ⓑ Ⓒ Ⓓ

HUMAN BODY

LEARNING OBJECTIVES

➤ The structure and function of nervous system
➤ The structure and function of heart and liver
➤ The mechanism of respiratory system

MULTIPLE CHOICE QUESTIONS

Direction: Select the correct option for each of the following questions.

1. Look at the diagram and answer the following questions.

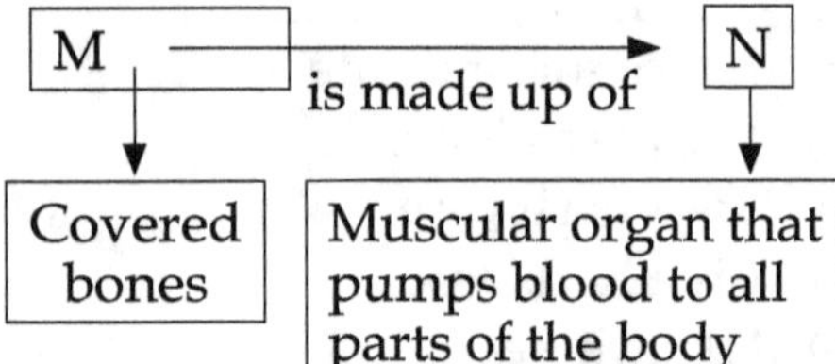

Which of the following are the most suitable terms for M and N?

	M	**N**
(A)	Skull	Brain
(B)	Ribcage	Brain
(C)	Pelvis	Heart
(D)	Ribcage	Heart

2. The function of molar teeth can be best illustrated by the function of __________.
   (A) Scissors
   (B) Mortar and pestle
   (C) Fork
   (D) Hammer

3. Which of the statements are not correct?
   (A) Eat meals at regular intervals for better digestion.
   (B) We should eat raw food for good health.
   (C) We should eat the same kind of food.
   (D) Eating stale food is good for health.

4. The respiratory system in humans consists of __________.
   (A) Nose, heart, lungs
   (B) Heart, lungs, wind pipe
   (C) Nose, lungs, wind pipe
   (D) Nose, heart

5. Which system do kidneys belong to __________.
   (A) Digestion   (B) Respiratory
   (C) Circulatory   (D) Excretory

6. Soni got injured and her friend gave her an immediate first-aid treatment. She was made to lie down with her legs raised so that her head was lower than her body. Soni most likely __________.
   (A) Got an electric shock
   (B) Fainted
   (C) Got an insect bite
   (D) Got burned

7. Which part of our body regulates our walking, talking, eating, etc.?
   (A) Nose   (B) Skin
   (C) Brain   (D) Heart

8. Which of the following activities will increase our heart rate?
   (A) Running   (B) Sitting
   (C) Standing   (D) Walking

9. The following diagram represents an organ, which takes in oxygen and gives out carbon dioxide. Name the organ.

| Organ | ⟵ Oxygen |
| | ⟶ Carbon dioxide |

   (A) Stomach
   (B) Lungs
   (C) Small intestine
   (D) Kidney

10. The inner layer of the stomach releases __________.
   (A) Minerals
   (B) Water
   (C) Digestive juices
   (D) Blood

11. Digested food is absorbed by __________.
   (A) Blood   (B) Water
   (C) Heart   (D) Lungs

12. Digested food is absorbed by blood in the __________.
   (A) Heart   (B) Lungs
   (C) Small intestine   (D) Stomach

13. In the figure given below, urine is stored in __________.

   (A) S   (B) R
   (C) P   (D) Q

14. Blood in our body is filtered by the __________.
   (A) Heart   (B) Veins
   (C) Blood vessels   (D) Kidney

15. Which of the following organs is bean-shaped?
   (A) Stomach   (B) Lungs
   (C) Kidney   (D) Heart

16. Which of the following systems is responsible for controlling all activities in the human body?
   (A) Nervous system
   (B) Respiratory system
   (C) Excretory system
   (D) Circulatory system

17. The two lower chambers of the heart are called __________.
   (A) Aorata   (B) Urethra
   (C) Auricles   (D) Ventricles

18. Digestion is completed in the __________.
   (A) Large intestine
   (B) Food pipe
   (C) Stomach
   (D) Small intestine

19. Undigested solid waste is excreted through:
   (A) Anus   (B) Large intestine
   (C) Skin   (D) Kidney

20. An adult has __________ teeth.
   (A) 20   (B) 24
   (C) 32   (D) 28

21. Which of the following is not true for the care of teeth?
   (A) We should not chew the food
   (B) We should eat raw fruits and vegetables
   (C) We should brush twice a day
   (D) We should not eat too many sweets

22. The blood flows to different parts of the body through __________.
   (A) Nerves
   (B) Tissues
   (C) Blood vessels
   (D) None of the above

23. The number of premolars in each jaw is __________.
    (A) 2   (B) 3
    (C) 5   (D) 4

24. The number of teeth in a three-month old baby is __________.
    (A) 12   (B) 32
    (C) 28   (D) None

25. In the below diagram, the teeth marked I represent __________.

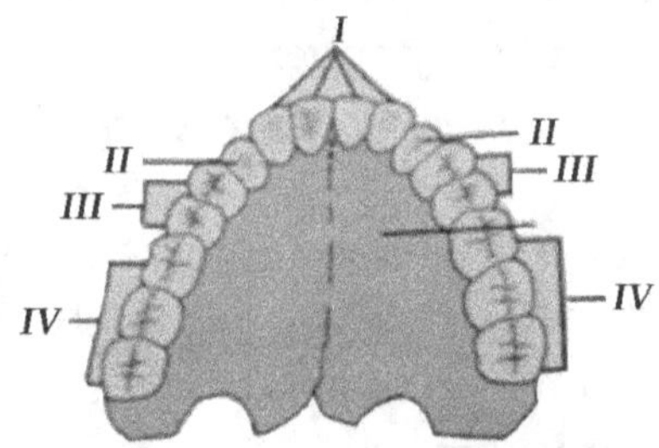

    (A) Incisor   (B) Premolar
    (C) Canines   (D) Molar

26. In the above diagram, the teeth marked III are also called __________.

    (A) Tearing teeth
    (B) Cracking teeth
    (C) Canines
    (D) Molar

27. In the above diagram, the teeth marked II represent __________.
    (A) Incisor   (B) Premolar
    (C) Canines   (D) Molar

28. The outer portion of the tooth above the gum line is called __________.
    (A) Pulp   (B) Root
    (C) Crown   (D) Enamel

29. Wisdom teeth appear at the age of __________.
    (A) 12–12 years   (B) 2–3 years
    (C) 20–25 years   (D) 13–16 years

30. Which kind of teeth is well developed in herbivores?
    (A) Incisors   (B) Molar
    (C) Canines   (D) Premolars

HOTS (ACHIEVERS SECTION)

31. The given figure shows the structure of a tooth. Select the correct option for the parts labelled P, Q, and R.

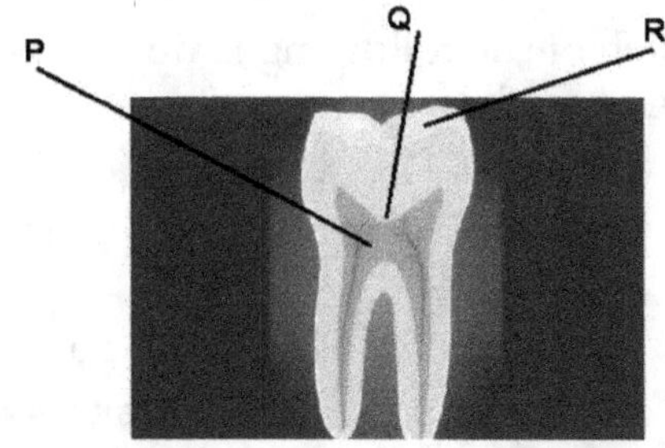

    (A) P has nerves and blood vessels.
    (B) R is the hardest substance of our body.
    (C) Q is the bone-like material that supports R.
    (D) All of these

32. What are the functions of the nervous system?

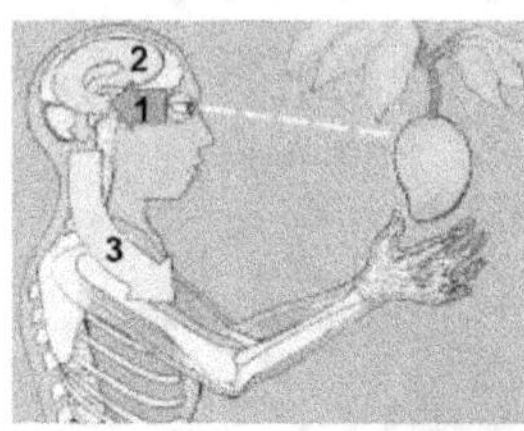

    I.   In the figure, number 3 signifies?
    II. In the figure, number 2 signifies?

	I	II
(A)	Motor output	Integration
(B)	Integration	Motor output
(C)	Sensory input	Integration
(D)	All of the above	Motor output

OLYMPIAD WORKBOOK (NSO) CLASS – 4

33. Which of the following is not a part of our Circulatory System?
  (A) Pancreas   (B) Arteries
  (C) Veins   (D) Capillaries

34. The inner layer of the stomach releases:
  (A) Minerals
  (B) Water
  (C) Digestive juices
  (D) Blood

35. Match the following:

[A] Incisors	(I) cracking teeth
[B] Canines	(II) cutting teeth
[C] Premolars	(III) grinding teeth
[D] Molars	(IV) tearing teeth

  (A) (A - III), (B - I), (C - IV), (D - II)
  (B) (A - IV), (B - III), (C - II), (D - I)
  (C) (A - II), (B - I), (C - IV), (D - III)
  (D) (A - II), (B - IV), (C - I), (D - III)
  (E) None of these

1. Ⓐ Ⓑ Ⓒ Ⓓ	8. Ⓐ Ⓑ Ⓒ Ⓓ	15. Ⓐ Ⓑ Ⓒ Ⓓ	22 Ⓐ Ⓑ Ⓒ Ⓓ	29. Ⓐ Ⓑ Ⓒ Ⓓ
2. Ⓐ Ⓑ Ⓒ Ⓓ	9. Ⓐ Ⓑ Ⓒ Ⓓ	16. Ⓐ Ⓑ Ⓒ Ⓓ	23. Ⓐ Ⓑ Ⓒ Ⓓ	30. Ⓐ Ⓑ Ⓒ Ⓓ
3. Ⓐ Ⓑ Ⓒ Ⓓ	10. Ⓐ Ⓑ Ⓒ Ⓓ	17. Ⓐ Ⓑ Ⓒ Ⓓ	24. Ⓐ Ⓑ Ⓒ Ⓓ	31. Ⓐ Ⓑ Ⓒ Ⓓ
4. Ⓐ Ⓑ Ⓒ Ⓓ	11. Ⓐ Ⓑ Ⓒ Ⓓ	18. Ⓐ Ⓑ Ⓒ Ⓓ	25. Ⓐ Ⓑ Ⓒ Ⓓ	32. Ⓐ Ⓑ Ⓒ Ⓓ
5. Ⓐ Ⓑ Ⓒ Ⓓ	12. Ⓐ Ⓑ Ⓒ Ⓓ	19. Ⓐ Ⓑ Ⓒ Ⓓ	26. Ⓐ Ⓑ Ⓒ Ⓓ	33. Ⓐ Ⓑ Ⓒ Ⓓ
6. Ⓐ Ⓑ Ⓒ Ⓓ	13. Ⓐ Ⓑ Ⓒ Ⓓ	20. Ⓐ Ⓑ Ⓒ Ⓓ	27. Ⓐ Ⓑ Ⓒ Ⓓ	34. Ⓐ Ⓑ Ⓒ Ⓓ
7. Ⓐ Ⓑ Ⓒ Ⓓ	14. Ⓐ Ⓑ Ⓒ Ⓓ	21. Ⓐ Ⓑ Ⓒ Ⓓ	28. Ⓐ Ⓑ Ⓒ Ⓓ	35. Ⓐ Ⓑ Ⓒ Ⓓ

FOOD, HEALTH AND SANITATION

LEARNING OBJECTIVES

➤ Food and nutrition
➤ Importance of preventive measures of various diseases
➤ Importance of proteins and nutrition

MULTIPLE CHOICE QUESTIONS

Direction: Select the correct option for each of the following questions.

1. Which of the following is a rich source of protein?
   (A) Coconut   (B) Egg
   (C) Tomato   (D) Bread

2. Lack of which nutrient can lead to goitre?
   (A) Iron   (B) Sodium
   (C) Iodine   (D) Calcium

3. For the Independence Day competition, Sonu was practising running. To get quick energy, which of the following nurtient-rich foods should he take?
   (A) Minerals   (B) Proteins
   (C) Fats   (D) Carbohydrates

4. Which of the following is not classified as food?
   (A) Oxygen   (B) Mineral water
   (C) Soft drinks   (D) Milk

5. Glucose, lactose, fructose, and starch belong to which group?
   (A) Fats   (B) Carbohydrates
   (C) Proteins   (D) Vitamins

6. I am a food item. I am added to Indian dishes to make them more appealing and tasty. I impact colour, flavour, and aroma of the dishes. Who am I?
   (A) Herbs   (B) Spices
   (C) Salt   (D) Sugar

7. Which component of food helps to get rid of undigested food from our body?
   (A) Roughage   (B) Vitamins
   (C) Proteins   (D) Fats

8. Aashu is a class 4 student. One day when he was playing with his friends, he saw an old man eating sugarcane with ease. Next day, he also tried to eat sugarcane but his teeth were paining and he was unable to eat. What is required for strong bones and teeth?
   (A) Fats   (B) Minerals
   (C) Vitamins   (D) Proteins

9. Oils, sweets, and ghee are a rich source of __________.
   (A) Carbohydrates   (B) Fats
   (C) Protein   (D) Vitamins

10. Sonia is a very lean 3-year-old girl. She has a swollen belly. Her skin is very dry. She eats chapaties and jaggery only. She could be a patient of __________.
    (A) PEM   (B) Malaria
    (C) Tuberculosis   (D) Rickets

11. Food items rich in vitamins and minerals are essential because __________.

(A) They keep our body warm.
(B) They give us energy.
(C) They fight disease and make our bones stronger.
(D) They build the cells in our body.

12. Which of the following components are needed in small quantities?
(A) Fats
(B) Carbohydrates
(C) Proteins
(D) Vitamins

13. Mr. Sam is suffering from blood pressure and heart diseases because of his obesity. Which of the following foods is causing this?
(A) Rice and wheat
(B) Green leafy vegetables
(C) Fats and oils
(D) Pulses

14. Which of the following has the highest amount of energy in them?
(A) Carbohydrates
(B) Fats
(C) Vitamins
(D) Minerals

15. Which of the following are essential for the formation and maintenance of bones?
(A) Vitamin D, iodine and glucose
(B) Calcium, phosphorous and vitamin D
(C) Phosphorous, fats and starch
(D) Calcium, iron and sodium

16. Boiling of milk __________.
(A) Kills the germs
(B) Improves taste
(C) Is not good for health
(D) Gives us more energy

17. Shelf life of food is related to __________.
(A) Freshness of food
(B) Quality of food
(C) Decomposition of food
(D) Time limit during which food can be consumed

18. Which of the following will not help to arrest the action of micro-organisms on tomatoes?
(A) Putting them in boiling water
(B) Putting them in the freezer
(C) Leaving them on the shelf
(D) None of these

19. Oil in pickles __________.
(A) Delays the action of micro-organisms
(B) Kills the micro-organisms
(C) Stops the action of micro-organisms
(D) Stops the action of enzymes

20. Freezing preserves food because it __________.
(A) Delays the action of micro-organisms
(B) Kills the micro-organisms
(C) Stops the action of micro-organisms
(D) Stops the action of enzymes

21. Which is a communicable disease?
(A) Polio
(B) Night blindness
(C) Chicken pox
(D) Rickets

22. Animal dung and other decaying matter can be used to produce:
(A) Manure
(B) Fertilizers
(C) Biogas
(D) Both (A) and (C)

23. Germs present in water can be killed by __________.
(A) Condensation
(B) Boiling
(C) Filteration
(D) Decantation

24. ORS means __________.
(A) Oral Regressive Solution
(B) Original Respiratory Syndrome
(C) Oral Rehydration Solution
(D) Operation Respiratory Solution

25. Loss of excess water and salt from the body is called __________.
(A) Perspiration
(B) Rehydration
(C) Dehydration
(D) Respiration

26. Which of the following diseases is caused because of unclean surroundings and bad food habits?
(A) Diarrhoea
(B) Cancer
(C) AIDS
(D) Small pox

27. By recycling __________.
(A) We can control pollution.
(B) We can save natural resources.
(C) We can make useful things from waste material.
(D) All of these

28. Organic waste can be disposed of by
    __________.
    (A) Compost pit   (B) Drain
    (C) Incineration   (D) None of these
29. To protect ourselves from diseases,
    sewage should be disposed off in _______.
    (A) Dustbins
    (B) Covered drainage system
    (C) Soakpit
    (D) Garbage dump
30. Which of the following vitamins is
    prepared in our body with the help of
    sunlight?
    (A) Vitamin A   (B) Vitamin B
    (C) Vitamin D   (D) Vitamin K

HOTS (ACHIEVERS SECTION)

31. Ananya's father was suffering from constipation. He visited the doctor. The doctor advised him to take a good amount of water and to include a good amount of roughage in his diet.
    I.   What is roughage?
    II. Why did the doctor recommend to include roughage in his diet?
    III. How many glasses of water should a healthy adult consume?
    IV. What are the sources of roughage?

	I	II	III	IV
(A)	Plant foods such as fruits and vegetables contain carbohydrates that cannot be digested by the body.	It is high-fibre food.	6–8	Citrus fruits
(B)	It is undigested food.	Roughage includes bulk in our diet, which ensures proper bowel movement.	5	Oranges and Amla
(C)	Digestible carbohydrates.	It adds bulk to our food. Since it is not digested, it passes down the entire digestive tract from the mouth to the anus.	7–8	Tomatoes, amla, green leafy vegetables, citrus fruits
(D)	Plant food such as fruits and vegetables contains carbohydrate that cannot be digested by the body. It is undigested food.	It adds bulk to our food. Since it is not digested, it passes down the entire digestive tract from the mouth to the anus.	6–8	Tomatoes, amla, green leafy vegetables, citrus fruits, and whole grains

32. Select the correct match:

	Nutrient		Source		Deficiency disease
A	Proteins	1	Bread	W	Scurvy
B	Fats	2	Green leafy vegetables	X	Kwashiorkor
C	Carbohydrates	3	Butter	Y	Weakness
D	Vitamins C	4	Egg yolk	Z	Marasmus

(A) A-4-X; B-3-Z; C-1-Y; D-2-W
(B) A-3-X; C-1-W; D-2-Y; B-3-Z
(C) A-4-Y; B-2-X; C-3-Z; D-1-W
(D) A-2-X; B-3-Z; C-1-Y; D-4-W

33. Which of the following teeth function in the same way as the object shown in the picture?
(A) Incisors
(B) Canines
(C) Molars
(D) Both (A) and (B)

34. Dehydration is a method of preserving food by
(A) Adding sugar   (B) Drying
(C) Adding salt   (D) Boiling

35. ______ is the method used to cook Pizza.
(A) Steaming   (B) Frying
(C) Boiling   (D) Baking

1.	Ⓐ Ⓑ Ⓒ Ⓓ	8.	Ⓐ Ⓑ Ⓒ Ⓓ	15.	Ⓐ Ⓑ Ⓒ Ⓓ	22	Ⓐ Ⓑ Ⓒ Ⓓ	29.	Ⓐ Ⓑ Ⓒ Ⓓ
2.	Ⓐ Ⓑ Ⓒ Ⓓ	9.	Ⓐ Ⓑ Ⓒ Ⓓ	16.	Ⓐ Ⓑ Ⓒ Ⓓ	23.	Ⓐ Ⓑ Ⓒ Ⓓ	30.	Ⓐ Ⓑ Ⓒ Ⓓ
3.	Ⓐ Ⓑ Ⓒ Ⓓ	10.	Ⓐ Ⓑ Ⓒ Ⓓ	17.	Ⓐ Ⓑ Ⓒ Ⓓ	24.	Ⓐ Ⓑ Ⓒ Ⓓ	31.	Ⓐ Ⓑ Ⓒ Ⓓ
4.	Ⓐ Ⓑ Ⓒ Ⓓ	11.	Ⓐ Ⓑ Ⓒ Ⓓ	18.	Ⓐ Ⓑ Ⓒ Ⓓ	25.	Ⓐ Ⓑ Ⓒ Ⓓ	32.	Ⓐ Ⓑ Ⓒ Ⓓ
5.	Ⓐ Ⓑ Ⓒ Ⓓ	12.	Ⓐ Ⓑ Ⓒ Ⓓ	19.	Ⓐ Ⓑ Ⓒ Ⓓ	26.	Ⓐ Ⓑ Ⓒ Ⓓ	33.	Ⓐ Ⓑ Ⓒ Ⓓ
6.	Ⓐ Ⓑ Ⓒ Ⓓ	13.	Ⓐ Ⓑ Ⓒ Ⓓ	20.	Ⓐ Ⓑ Ⓒ Ⓓ	27.	Ⓐ Ⓑ Ⓒ Ⓓ	34.	Ⓐ Ⓑ Ⓒ Ⓓ
7.	Ⓐ Ⓑ Ⓒ Ⓓ	14.	Ⓐ Ⓑ Ⓒ Ⓓ	21.	Ⓐ Ⓑ Ⓒ Ⓓ	28.	Ⓐ Ⓑ Ⓒ Ⓓ	35.	Ⓐ Ⓑ Ⓒ Ⓓ

HUMAN NEEDS

LEARNING OBJECTIVES

- ➤ Clothes
- ➤ Different sources of fibres
- ➤ Various types of shelters
- ➤ The process from fibre to fabric
- ➤ Different properties of fabrics

MULTIPLE CHOICE QUESTIONS

Direction: Select the correct option for each of the following questions.

1. Clothes are mainly used __________.
   - (A) To cover the body
   - (B) To be attractive
   - (C) For comfort and protection
   - (D) All of these

2. Eskimos use __________.
   - (A) Helmets
   - (B) Bullet proofs
   - (C) Robes
   - (D) Fur

3. Insignias mean __________.
   - (A) Decoration
   - (B) Badges
   - (C) Uniforms
   - (D) Fur

4. Football players wear __________.
   - (A) Asbestos clothing
   - (B) Fur
   - (C) Protective padding
   - (D) Robes

5. Cotton is stronger when it is wet. This is because __________.
   - (A) It contains crystalline fibre.
   - (B) It is hydrophilic in nature.
   - (C) It has a cellulose layer.
   - (D) All of these

6. Cotton plant is __________.
   - (A) Lengthy
   - (B) Shallow
   - (C) Bushy
   - (D) Hard

7. Cotton buds blossom in __________.
   - (A) 21 days
   - (B) 23 days
   - (C) 20 days
   - (D) 24 days

8. The moisture absorption is __________.
   - (A) 8%
   - (B) 9.5%
   - (C) 8.5%
   - (D) 6%

9. Which of these fibres is/are strong and lustrous?
   - (A) Cotton
   - (B) Silk
   - (C) Linen
   - (D) Wool

10. The silk fibre was invented by __________.
    - (A) Egyptians
    - (B) Japanese
    - (C) Indians
    - (D) Chinese

11. In which century were synthetic yarns introduced?
    - (A) 10th
    - (B) 20th
    - (C) 16th
    - (D) 19th

12. Artificial silk is __________.
    - (A) Rayon
    - (B) Polyester
    - (C) Acrylic
    - (D) Acetate

13. Polyester is referred to as _______.
   (A) Dupont
   (B) Work horse
   (C) Cellulose acetate
   (D) Acrylic

14. An important tool in taking body measurement is _______.
   (A) Scale
   (B) Measuring tape
   (C) Tracing wheel
   (D) Thread

15. Existing weather conditions determine the _______.
   (A) Material used for the house in an area.
   (B) Shape of the house in an area.
   (C) Design of the house in an area.
   (D) All of these

16. Slanting roofs _______.
   (A) Do not collect snow and rain water
   (B) Collect rain water
   (C) Collect snow
   (D) Keep the house hot and warm

17. Bricks are baked in _______.
   (A) Furnaces
   (B) Kilns
   (C) Electric oven
   (D) Open furnaces

18. An elevated house on bamboo poles is usually made in places _______.
   (A) Where it is very warm
   (B) Where it snows
   (C) Where floods occur due to heavy rains
   (D) Where there is fear of theft

19. In Japan houses are usually made of wood because _______.
   (A) It is very cheap
   (B) Of frequent earthquakes
   (C) It is cool inside a wooden house
   (D) The Japanese are nomadic

20. To protect the house from the influence of weather, it should be coated with _______.
   (A) Paint
   (B) Dung cake
   (C) Spray of kerosene
   (D) Mud and straw

21. *Kuccha* houses are built with _______.
   (A) Concrete
   (B) Cement
   (C) Baled bricks
   (D) Unbaked bricks

22. *Pucca* houses are built with _______.
   (A) Unbaked bricks
   (B) Baked bricks
   (C) Mud and straw
   (D) Ice and straw

23. Igloos are constructed with _______.
   (A) Ice
   (B) Mud and straw
   (C) Baked bricks
   (D) Cement, bricks, and gravel

24. The windows should be in the opposite direction to the door _______.
   (A) To let more light enter the house
   (B) To move easily
   (C) To facilitate cross ventilation
   (D) To have a good view of surroundings

25. A high roof in a house _______.
   (A) Is good for rains
   (B) Keeps it warm in winter
   (C) Keeps it cold in summer
   (D) All of these

26. Synthetic fibres are obtained from
    (A) plants   (B) sheep
    (C) silkworm   (D) chemicals

27. Which of the following is most suitable for making umbrellas?
    (A) Cotton
    (B) Woollen
    (C) Water proof materials
    (D) Water absorbing materials

28. Bleaching and dyeing are usually done
    (A) just before the fabrics are made.
    (B) just before the yarns are made.
    (C) after the fabrics are made.
    (D) after the yarns are made.

29. Which of the following materials is wrongly grouped in the chart below?

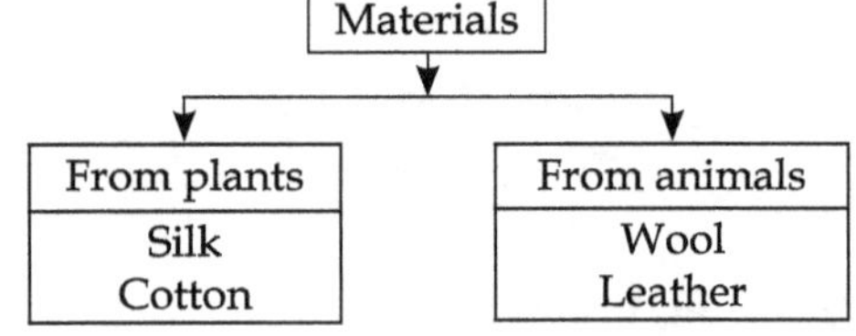

    (A) Wool   (B) Silk
    (C) Cotton   (D) Leather

30. Seema uses a certain coat in very cold weather. The coat she chooses should be made of
    (A) cotton   (B) wool
    (C) silk   (D) plastic

1.	Ⓐ Ⓑ Ⓒ Ⓓ	7.	Ⓐ Ⓑ Ⓒ Ⓓ	13.	Ⓐ Ⓑ Ⓒ Ⓓ	19	Ⓐ Ⓑ Ⓒ Ⓓ	25.	Ⓐ Ⓑ Ⓒ Ⓓ
2.	Ⓐ Ⓑ Ⓒ Ⓓ	8.	Ⓐ Ⓑ Ⓒ Ⓓ	14.	Ⓐ Ⓑ Ⓒ Ⓓ	20.	Ⓐ Ⓑ Ⓒ Ⓓ	26.	Ⓐ Ⓑ Ⓒ Ⓓ
3.	Ⓐ Ⓑ Ⓒ Ⓓ	9.	Ⓐ Ⓑ Ⓒ Ⓓ	15.	Ⓐ Ⓑ Ⓒ Ⓓ	21.	Ⓐ Ⓑ Ⓒ Ⓓ	27.	Ⓐ Ⓑ Ⓒ Ⓓ
4.	Ⓐ Ⓑ Ⓒ Ⓓ	10.	Ⓐ Ⓑ Ⓒ Ⓓ	16.	Ⓐ Ⓑ Ⓒ Ⓓ	22.	Ⓐ Ⓑ Ⓒ Ⓓ	28.	Ⓐ Ⓑ Ⓒ Ⓓ
5.	Ⓐ Ⓑ Ⓒ Ⓓ	11.	Ⓐ Ⓑ Ⓒ Ⓓ	17.	Ⓐ Ⓑ Ⓒ Ⓓ	23.	Ⓐ Ⓑ Ⓒ Ⓓ	29.	Ⓐ Ⓑ Ⓒ Ⓓ
6.	Ⓐ Ⓑ Ⓒ Ⓓ	12.	Ⓐ Ⓑ Ⓒ Ⓓ	18.	Ⓐ Ⓑ Ⓒ Ⓓ	24.	Ⓐ Ⓑ Ⓒ Ⓓ	30.	Ⓐ Ⓑ Ⓒ Ⓓ

MATTER AND MATERIALS 

LEARNING OBJECTIVES

➤ The compositions of matter
➤ Different states of matter and their inter conversion
➤ Mixtures, their types and methods of separation

MULTIPLE CHOICE QUESTIONS

Direction: Select the correct option for each of the following questions.

1. The amount of space taken up by matter is called —————.
   (A) Volume
   (B) Shape
   (C) Mass
   (D) Width

2. Which of the following is/are in a liquid state normally?
   (A) Mercury
   (B) Water
   (C) Petrol
   (D) All of these

3. Which of the following states of matter has the strongest forces of attraction between its molecules?
   (A) Solid　　　　(B) Liquid
   (C) Gas　　　　(D) None

4. The bubbles that come out rapidly when we open a soda water bottle are —————.
   (A) Water bubbles
   (B) Nitrogen bubbles
   (C) Oxygen bubbles
   (D) Carbon dioxide bubbles

5. Which of the following can vary in volume?

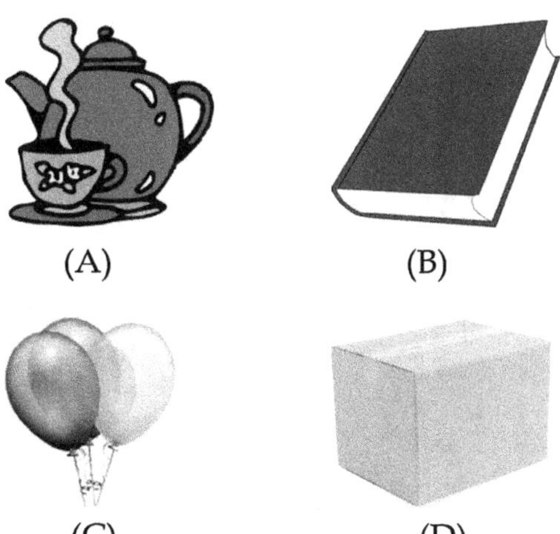

6. Which of the following has a fixed volume but no fixed shape?
   (A) Water vapour
   (B) Salt
   (C) Milk
   (D) Ice

7. Three different containers shown below contain 500 ml of water in each of them.

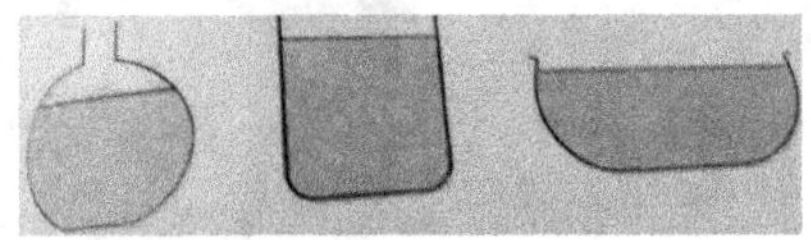

This indicates that water has __________
(A) No definite shape
(B) A definite volume
(C) No definite volume
(D) A definite shape

8. Which of the following is not solid?
(A) Plasticine   (B) Flour
(C) Cotton wool   (D) Honey

9. We can separate sand from water by __________.
(A) Boiling   (B) Evaporation
(C) Filtration   (D) Condensation

10. Sunil took some water and dissolved some salt in it. Later he placed the salty water under sunlight for four days. He found only the crystals of salt but not the water. The process demonstrated in the above experiment is __________.
(A) Condensation   (B) Filtration
(C) Boiling   (D) Evaporation

11. Look at the given pictures carefully. They show particles of the same matter. In which picture is the matter coldest?

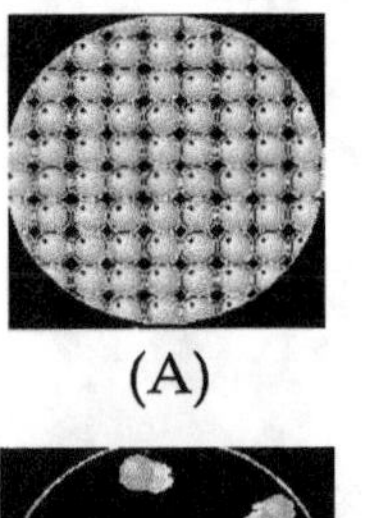
(A)

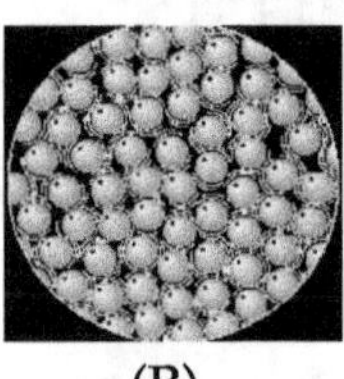
(B)

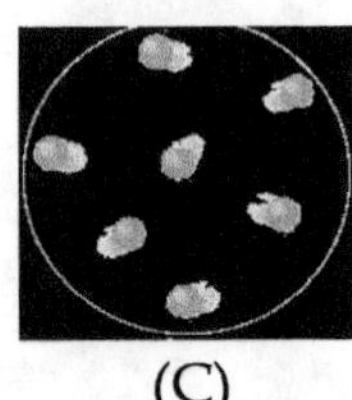
(C)

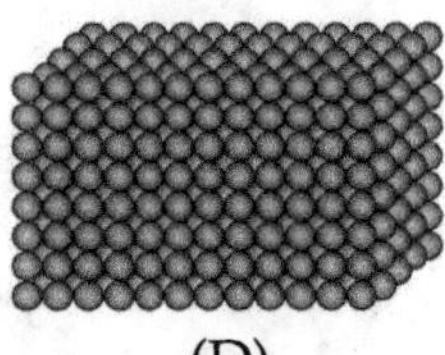
(D)

12. Which of the following is incorrectly written?
(A) The bag of flour weighs 10 kg
(B) The chocolate weighs 20 gm
(C) The capacity of the jug is 2 litres
(D) The capacity of the water tank is 1 kg

13. The object in the given figure is made of a combination of __________ and __________.

(A) Wood, metal
(B) Metal, plastic
(C) Rubber, wood
(D) Glass, metal

14. Which of the following objects is incorrectly classified?

Do not allow light to pass through	Allow some light to pass through	Allow light to pass through
Cardboard	Tracing paper	Glass
Wood	Metal can	Clean water

(A) Tracing paper   (B) Metal can
(C) Clean water   (D) Wood

15. Air is different from water; it __________.
(A) Has no definite volume
(B) Has a definite mass
(C) Has no definite shape
(D) Occupies space

16. The homogeneous mixture of two or more substances is called __________.
(A) Mixture   (B) Solute
(C) Solvent   (D) Solution

17. Soda water contains dissolved __________.
(A) Carbon dioxide   (B) Oxygen
(C) Common salt   (D) Wax

18. When gas changes into liquid, it is called __________.
(A) Melting   (B) Solidification
(C) Evaporation   (D) Condensation

19. One day Surya's father put naphthalene balls between woolen clothes to keep them protected from insects. After a few days he saw that the size of the naphthalene balls had reduced. This process is called __________.
(A) Sublimation   (B) Condensation
(C) Melting   (D) Freezing

20. Look at the following picture carefully and find out which material the below object is made of?

(A) Wood   (B) Plastic
(C) Glass   (D) Metal

21. Name the solutes that are soluble in water?
(A) Sand and salt
(B) Sand and sugar
(C) Sugar and salt
(D) Salt and kerosene

22. Which of the following is an insoluble substance in water?
(A) Salt   (B) Oxygen
(C) Sand   (D) Sugar

23. When describing the colour, size, shape, or smell of an object, you are describing the __________.
(A) Physical Properties of matter
(B) States of matter
(C) Chemical properties of metter
(D) Mass of matter

24. A chemical change takes place when one form of matter changes to __________.
(A) An atom
(B) Another kind of matter
(C) A molecule
(D) None of these

25. Solids can keep their shape because __________.
(A) Particles in solids stay close together
(B) Particles in solids stay far apart
(C) Particles in solids are cold
(D) Particles in solids are hot

HOTS (ACHIEVERS SECTION)

26. Look at this picture of a mixture of sugar and water.

A student uses a hot plate to separate a mixture of water and sugar. Which physical property allows this to occur?
(A) Water's crystal-like structure
(B) Sugar's ability to evaporate
(C) Water's ability to evaporate
(D) Sugar's crystal-like structure

27. This diagram shows a light bulb. The bottom of the light bulb is shaped so that the bulb fits securely into a light socket.

I.   Which type of simple machine is the bottom of the bulb?
II. What is the shape of a filament in the light bulb?

	I	II
(A)	Lever	Coiled
(B)	Pulley	Straight
(C)	Screw	Coiled
(D)	Wedge	Straight

28. Chopping of wood is which kind of change?
    (A) Physical change
    (B) No change
    (C) Chemical change
    (D) Biological change

29. Which of the following is not a gaseous fuel?
    (A) CNG
    (B) Coal
    (C) LPG
    (D) Hydrogen

30. Pressure applied on solids, can change its:
    (A) Shape
    (B) Volume
    (C) Colour
    (D) Mass

————Darken Your Choice with HB Pencil————

1.	Ⓐ Ⓑ Ⓒ Ⓓ	7.	Ⓐ Ⓑ Ⓒ Ⓓ	13.	Ⓐ Ⓑ Ⓒ Ⓓ	19	Ⓐ Ⓑ Ⓒ Ⓓ	25.	Ⓐ Ⓑ Ⓒ Ⓓ
2.	Ⓐ Ⓑ Ⓒ Ⓓ	8.	Ⓐ Ⓑ Ⓒ Ⓓ	14.	Ⓐ Ⓑ Ⓒ Ⓓ	20.	Ⓐ Ⓑ Ⓒ Ⓓ	26.	Ⓐ Ⓑ Ⓒ Ⓓ
3.	Ⓐ Ⓑ Ⓒ Ⓓ	9.	Ⓐ Ⓑ Ⓒ Ⓓ	15.	Ⓐ Ⓑ Ⓒ Ⓓ	21.	Ⓐ Ⓑ Ⓒ Ⓓ	27.	Ⓐ Ⓑ Ⓒ Ⓓ
4.	Ⓐ Ⓑ Ⓒ Ⓓ	10.	Ⓐ Ⓑ Ⓒ Ⓓ	16.	Ⓐ Ⓑ Ⓒ Ⓓ	22.	Ⓐ Ⓑ Ⓒ Ⓓ	28.	Ⓐ Ⓑ Ⓒ Ⓓ
5.	Ⓐ Ⓑ Ⓒ Ⓓ	11.	Ⓐ Ⓑ Ⓒ Ⓓ	17.	Ⓐ Ⓑ Ⓒ Ⓓ	23.	Ⓐ Ⓑ Ⓒ Ⓓ	29.	Ⓐ Ⓑ Ⓒ Ⓓ
6.	Ⓐ Ⓑ Ⓒ Ⓓ	12.	Ⓐ Ⓑ Ⓒ Ⓓ	18.	Ⓐ Ⓑ Ⓒ Ⓓ	24.	Ⓐ Ⓑ Ⓒ Ⓓ	30.	Ⓐ Ⓑ Ⓒ Ⓓ

WORK, FORCE AND ENERGY 

LEARNING OBJECTIVES

- ➤ The concept of rest and motion
- ➤ Describe energy, its types and units
- ➤ Sound
- ➤ Force, action and reaction
- ➤ Energy conservation

MULTIPLE CHOICE QUESTIONS

1. Choose the wrong statement among followings.
   - (A) Sounds vary in three ways: volume (loud or soft), pitch (high or low), and timbre (quality).
   - (B) The loudness of sound is measured in decibels (dB).
   - (C) Acoustics is the science and technology of energy.
   - (D) All of the above statements are incorrect.

2. In which of the following situations no work is done?
   - (A) A spaceship moves at constant velocity.
   - (B) A child slides down a playground slide.
   - (C) You push on a heavy box but cannot move it.
   - (D) You slam on the brakes and your car stops quickly.

3. The following is a diagram of a simple electromagnet.

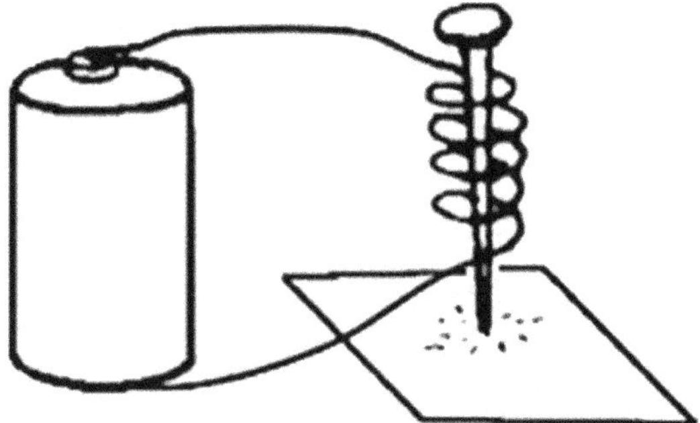

Simple Electro-magnet

How could this electromagnet be made stronger?
   - (A) Remove all the coils and the nail.
   - (B) Add more coils of wire to the nail.
   - (C) Use a smaller battery.
   - (D) Reverse the poles of the magnet.

4. An __________ travels faster than sound.
   - (A) Fighter plane
   - (B) Aircraft
   - (C) Supersonic jet
   - (D) All of these

5. Why we sprinkle talcum powder on a carrom board?
   (A) To reduce frictional force
   (B) To reduce gravitational force
   (C) To reduce elastic force
   (D) To reduce muscular energy

6. Look at the following picture carefully. First identify the picture. The below machine is a combination of three simple machines. Which simple machines combine to make it?

   (A) Pulley and lever
   (B) Lever and gears
   (C) Wheel, axle and gears
   (D) Gears

7. Electricity travelling through a wire is an example of __________.
   (A) A force applied by a simple machine.
   (B) Energy flowing through the water cycle.
   (C) Earth's gravitational pull on an object.
   (D) Energy being transferred from place to place.

8. Rahul is applying force on a moving object in the same direction, the speed of the object __________.
   (A) Remains the same
   (B) Increases
   (C) Decreases
   (D) Sometime decreases and sometime increases

9. When we throw a ball into the air, it falls back. The force responsible for this is __________.
   (A) Mechanical force
   (B) Muscular force
   (C) Friction force
   (D) Gravitational force

10. In which of these activities, the sense of hearing is least important?

    (A)    (B) 

    (C)    (D) 

11. Two girls are playing table tennis. First girl hit the ball over the net and at a Point say 'T', the other girl hit it back with a lot of force.

    What would happen at point 'T'?
    i.   The force caused a change in the size of the ball.
    ii. The force caused a change in the direction of the ball.
    iii. The force caused the ball to stop moving.
    (A) i
    (B) ii
    (C) Both i and ii
    (D) Both i and iii

12. Air pressure is measured with an __________.
    (A) Thermometer
    (B) Barometer
    (C) Anemometer
    (D) Psychrometer

13. These products of nature are such as coal and oil are __________, which means that when they are gone, nature cannot make them again. It is very important to limit their use and find other resources to replace them.

(A) Usable   (B) Replaceable
(C) Non-renewable   (D) Unlimited

14. The _____________ works by using fuel derived from living and dead biological organisms.
(A) Wind Energy   (B) Solar Energy
(C) Hydroelectric   (D) Biofuel

15. Look at the lever below.

Which object has the similar working principle as the above lever?

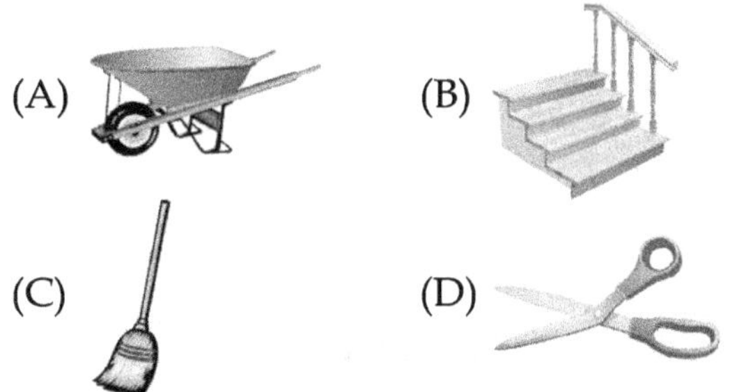

(A)   (B)   (C)   (D)

16. While walking, which of the following types of energy and work are involved?
(A) Mechanical and kinetic energies
(B) Potential energy and the work done by the force that moves the body
(C) Kinetic energy, potential energy, work done by forces excluding the body's weight and work lost through friction
(D) Kinetic energy, potential energy and work done by the body's weight

17. What happens to the total energy of a moving object if all the applied forces are conserved?
(A) It increases
(B) It decreases
(C) It remains constant
(D) The velocity is required to answer this question

18. Mark the action in which work is being done _____________
(A) Carrying a rucksack to school.
(B) A vehicle warming up its motor.
(C) A computer running a program.
(D) A man trying to open the door.

19. As defined in physics, work is done _____________.
(A) When an object moves
(B) When an object is stationary
(C) When an object stops
(D) Both (A) and (C)

20. If the resultant force acting on a body of constant mass is zero, the body's momentum is _____________.
(A) Increasing   (B) Decreasing
(C) Always zero   (D) Constant

21. Which of the following gadget is used to measure temperature?
(A) Stop watch
(B) Scale
(C) Measuring jar
(D) Thermometer

22. To measure the weight of milk, which of the following units can be used?
(A) Fahrenheit   (B) Millilitre
(C) Milligram   (D) Seconds

23. A calorimeter is used to _____________.
(A) Determine the heat of a reaction.
(B) Determine the heat given off/ absorbed during some process.
(C) Store the heat from a chemical reaction.
(D) None of these

24. What is nuclear energy?
(A) Energy that is from solar panels.
(B) Energy that is locked in the nucleus of an atom.
(C) The kinetic energy of moving electrons.
(D) Energy that travels in waves.

25. Blow at a plastic toy windmill and then hold it under a tap from which water is dripping. Which of the following, this activity is trying to show?
  (A) That tap and wind blown possess energy.
  (B) That wind and flowing water possess energy.
  (C) That moving air and moving water does not possess energy.
  (D) That only wind possesses energy.

26. As you go up a mountain top, your weight __________.
  (A) Increases slightly
  (B) Decreases slightly
  (C) Remains exactly the same
  (D) Increases sharply

27. Which of the following is NOT an SI unit of measure?
  (A) Watt   (B) Newton
  (C) Joule   (D) Hertz

28. Which of these contains an electromagnet?
  (A) Lamp
  (B) Electric stove
  (C) Compass
  (D) Headphones

29. The mechanical energy of a freely falling object is the difference __________.
  (A) Between its potential energy and its kinetic energy
  (B) Between its potential energy and its gravitational energy
  (C) Between its friction energy and its potential energy
  (D) None of these

30. The part of a nuclear power plant that prevents thermal pollution of lakes or rivers is the __________.
  (A) Reactor
  (B) Coolant/moderator
  (C) Cooling tower
  (D) Control rod

HOTS (ACHIEVERS SECTION)

31. Your mom is cooking a pot of spaghetti on the stove. You observe that the spaghetti moves all around the pot even though she is not stirring. What makes the spaghetti move?
  (A) It is the heat energy which causes the spaghetti to move.
  (B) All three forms of heat transfer are often working at the same time, making the spaghetti move.
  (C) Radiation energy causes the spaghetti to move.
  (D) The spaghetti is slippery in texture and it moves due to its texture.

32. Which graph represents an object that is decreasing in speed?

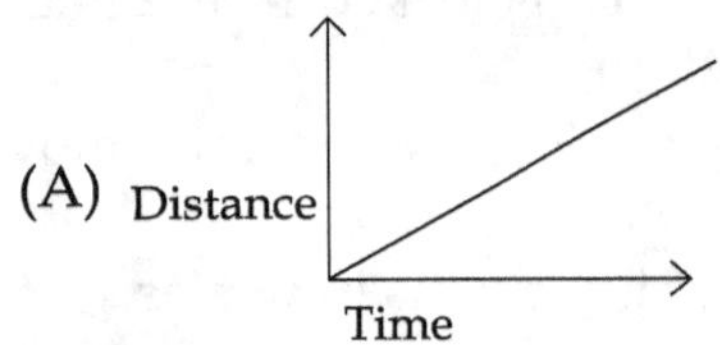

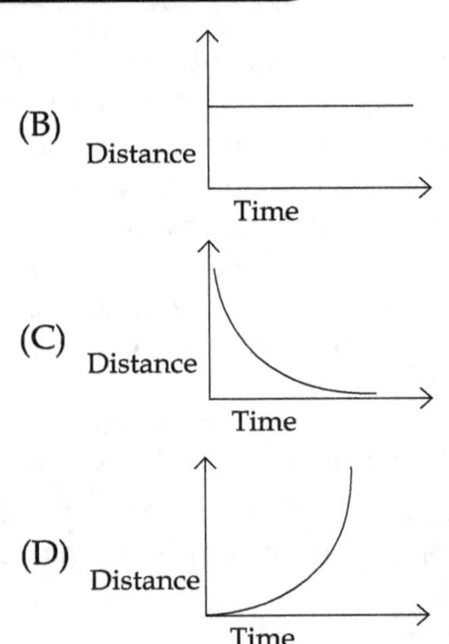

33. I. Which of these makes a sound with the slowest vibration?

   II. Which sound waves create noise?

	I	II
(A)	Drum	Irregular repetative sound waves
(B)	Whistle	Regularly repeating sound waves
(C)	Flute	High frequency sound waves
(D)	Harmonica	Low frequency sound waves

34. While writing with chalk on the blackboard, your teacher is able to write with the help of this force:
    (A) Gravitational force
    (B) Elastic force
    (C) Frictional force
    (D) Electrostatic force

35. Ankita is standing on the road, carrying a bag filled with vegetables, no work is done in this because:
    (A) Ankita is carrying a bag.
    (B) Ankita is not sitting.
    (C) There is not any change in the position of Ankita.
    (D) All the above

1. Ⓐ Ⓑ Ⓒ Ⓓ	8. Ⓐ Ⓑ Ⓒ Ⓓ	15. Ⓐ Ⓑ Ⓒ Ⓓ	22 Ⓐ Ⓑ Ⓒ Ⓓ	29. Ⓐ Ⓑ Ⓒ Ⓓ
2. Ⓐ Ⓑ Ⓒ Ⓓ	9. Ⓐ Ⓑ Ⓒ Ⓓ	16. Ⓐ Ⓑ Ⓒ Ⓓ	23. Ⓐ Ⓑ Ⓒ Ⓓ	30. Ⓐ Ⓑ Ⓒ Ⓓ
3. Ⓐ Ⓑ Ⓒ Ⓓ	10. Ⓐ Ⓑ Ⓒ Ⓓ	17. Ⓐ Ⓑ Ⓒ Ⓓ	24. Ⓐ Ⓑ Ⓒ Ⓓ	31. Ⓐ Ⓑ Ⓒ Ⓓ
4. Ⓐ Ⓑ Ⓒ Ⓓ	11. Ⓐ Ⓑ Ⓒ Ⓓ	18. Ⓐ Ⓑ Ⓒ Ⓓ	25. Ⓐ Ⓑ Ⓒ Ⓓ	32. Ⓐ Ⓑ Ⓒ Ⓓ
5. Ⓐ Ⓑ Ⓒ Ⓓ	12. Ⓐ Ⓑ Ⓒ Ⓓ	19. Ⓐ Ⓑ Ⓒ Ⓓ	26. Ⓐ Ⓑ Ⓒ Ⓓ	33. Ⓐ Ⓑ Ⓒ Ⓓ
6. Ⓐ Ⓑ Ⓒ Ⓓ	13. Ⓐ Ⓑ Ⓒ Ⓓ	20. Ⓐ Ⓑ Ⓒ Ⓓ	27. Ⓐ Ⓑ Ⓒ Ⓓ	34. Ⓐ Ⓑ Ⓒ Ⓓ
7. Ⓐ Ⓑ Ⓒ Ⓓ	14. Ⓐ Ⓑ Ⓒ Ⓓ	21. Ⓐ Ⓑ Ⓒ Ⓓ	28. Ⓐ Ⓑ Ⓒ Ⓓ	35. Ⓐ Ⓑ Ⓒ Ⓓ

OUR ENVIRONMENT

LEARNING OBJECTIVES

➤ Global warming
➤ Waste disposal
➤ Festivals and languages

MULTIPLE CHOICE QUESTIONS

1. What is Sewage?
   (A) Mining waste
   (B) Factory waste
   (C) Domestic waste
   (D) None of the above

2. The process of gradual increase in the earth's temperature is called________.
   (A) Pollution
   (B) Green house effect
   (C) Global warming
   (D) Acid rain

3. The Solid part of the Earth comprising rocks forms the
   (A) Lithosphere
   (B) Hydrosphere
   (C) Atmosphere
   (D) None of the above

4. The cutting down of trees on a large scale is called
   (A) afforestation
   (B) deforestation
   (C) both a and b
   (D) None of these

5. Non-biodegradable waste is one of the major cause of land pollution. Which one of the following is a better option to get rid of non- biodegradable waste?
   (A) Burning
   (B) Burying
   (C) Recycling
   (D) Dumping

6. The most important reason for ozone layer depletion is the production and emission of _________ which is used in refrigerator and air conditioners.
   (A) Ozone gas
   (B) Chlorofluoro Carbons
   (C) carbon-di-oxide
   (D) None of the above

7. Forests are called as the 'lungs of nature" why?
   (A) Bring down the carbon dioxide level in the atmosphere
   (B) Bring down the oxygen level in the atmosphere
   (C) Maintain the balance of oxygen and carbon dioxide in the atmosphere
   (D) Increase the level of carbon dioxide in the atmosphere

8. The whole mass of air surrounding the Earth is called
   (A) Hydrosphere
   (B) Atmosphere
   (C) Lithosphere
   (D) none of the above

9. Contamination unwanted substances into water is called _____.
   (A) Air pollution
   (B) Water pollution
   (C) Land pollution
   (D) Soil pollution

10. The _________ is the only planet in our Solar System known to have life.
   (A) Mars
   (B) Jupiter
   (C) Earth
   (D) venus

11. Which one of the following is a biotic component of the environment?
   (A) Water
   (B) Air
   (C) Land
   (D) Plant

12. _________ dominates the South Indian diet.
   (A) Wheat
   (B) Rice
   (C) Bajra
   (D) None of these

13. Acid rain causes damage to___________.
   (A) Animals life
   (B) Plants life
   (C) Historical monuments
   (D) All of these

14. Mahl and Portuguese are _________ languages.
   (A) Majority
   (B) Classical
   (C) Regional
   (D) Minority

15. Under which one of the following groups, pills of vegetable should be kept?
   (A) Hazardous
   (B) Non-biodegradable
   (C) Biodegradable
   (D) Toxic

16. _________ causes extinction of Wildlife by destroying their habitat.
   (A) afforestation
   (B) deforestation
   (C) both a and b
   (D) None of these

17. We, human beings, depend on our ____ for all our needs
   (A) Atmosphere
   (B) Environment
   (C) Lithosphere
   (D) Hydrosphere

18. Independence Day, Republic Day and Gandhi Jayanti are _________ festivals of India.
   (A) National
   (B) Religious
   (C) Harvest
   (D) None of these

19. Which are the official languages of central Governments?
   (A) Urdu and Hindi
   (B) Hindi and English
   (C) Both
   (D) None of these

20. Rajasthani, Bihari, Haryanvi are _________ languages.
   (A) Majority
   (B) Minority
   (C) Classical
   (D) Regional

21. Which statement among the following is not correct?
    (A) Dumping plastics in the soil causes soil pollution.
    (B) Loudspeakers, vehicles causes noise pollution.
    (C) Burning of garbage leads to air pollution.
    (D) Bathing animals in rivers makes water clean.

22. Match the following:

Column A	Column B
(I) Water pollution	[A] Dumping of solid waste in the soil
(II) Air pollution	[B] Honking
(III) Land pollution	[C] Sewage water into rivers
(IV) Noise pollution	[D] Fumes

    (A) (I-C), (II-D), (III-A), (IV-B)
    (B) (I-D), (II-C), (III-B), (IV-A)
    (C) (I-B), (II-A), (III-D), (IV-C)
    (D) (I-C), (II-A), (III-D), (IV-B)

23. Match the following;

Column A	Column B
(I) Typhoid	[A] Air
(II) Bronchitis	[B] Soil
(III) Deafness	[C] Water
(IV) Pesticides	[D] Noise

    (A) (I-B), (II-A), (III-D), (IV-C)
    (B) (I-D), (II-C), (III-A), (IV-B)
    (C) (I-C), (II-A), (III-D), (IV-B)
    (D) (I-C), (II-D), (III-B), (IV-A)

24. Unscramble the name of a tree which gives us a sour fruit?
    (A) ETDA   (B) ITLICH
    (C) NLMEO   (D) EAKT

25. Which among the following statements is correct?
    (A) We should use plastic bags more and more.
    (B) We should allow stagnated water to stand.
    (C) We should dispose of dry waste and wet waste separately.
    (D) We should use petrol at the place of CNG.

1.	Ⓐ Ⓑ Ⓒ Ⓓ	6.	Ⓐ Ⓑ Ⓒ Ⓓ	11.	Ⓐ Ⓑ Ⓒ Ⓓ	16	Ⓐ Ⓑ Ⓒ Ⓓ	21.	Ⓐ Ⓑ Ⓒ Ⓓ
2.	Ⓐ Ⓑ Ⓒ Ⓓ	7.	Ⓐ Ⓑ Ⓒ Ⓓ	12.	Ⓐ Ⓑ Ⓒ Ⓓ	17.	Ⓐ Ⓑ Ⓒ Ⓓ	22.	Ⓐ Ⓑ Ⓒ Ⓓ
3.	Ⓐ Ⓑ Ⓒ Ⓓ	8.	Ⓐ Ⓑ Ⓒ Ⓓ	13.	Ⓐ Ⓑ Ⓒ Ⓓ	18.	Ⓐ Ⓑ Ⓒ Ⓓ	23.	Ⓐ Ⓑ Ⓒ Ⓓ
4.	Ⓐ Ⓑ Ⓒ Ⓓ	9.	Ⓐ Ⓑ Ⓒ Ⓓ	14.	Ⓐ Ⓑ Ⓒ Ⓓ	19.	Ⓐ Ⓑ Ⓒ Ⓓ	23.	Ⓐ Ⓑ Ⓒ Ⓓ
5.	Ⓐ Ⓑ Ⓒ Ⓓ	10.	Ⓐ Ⓑ Ⓒ Ⓓ	15.	Ⓐ Ⓑ Ⓒ Ⓓ	20.	Ⓐ Ⓑ Ⓒ Ⓓ	25.	Ⓐ Ⓑ Ⓒ Ⓓ

EARTH AND UNIVERSE

LEARNING OBJECTIVES

➤ The solar system and other heavenly bodies
➤ The rotation of the earth on its axis
➤ Different patterns of major constellations

MULTIPLE CHOICE QUESTIONS

Direction: Select the correct option for each of the following questions.

1. A basketball spinning on someone's finger is _________.
   - (A) Rotation
   - (B) Revolution
   - (C) Half rotation
   - (D) Half revolution

2. Where on the earth do you think it would be easy to capture solar energy?
   - (A) The desert
   - (B) Near the equator
   - (C) Any place where it is sunny most of the time
   - (D) All of these

3. Part of the earth that supports life and where living beings exist is called ______.
   - (A) Atmosphere
   - (B) Biosphere
   - (C) Biology
   - (D) Biodiversity

4. Which planet is the only one that supports animal and plant life?
   - (A) Venus
   - (B) Earth
   - (C) Mars
   - (D) Pluto

5. A day on Venus is _________.
   - (A) Shorter than its year
   - (B) Very cold
   - (C) Longer than its year
   - (D) Very hot

6. The following planets are all made up of gas _________.
   - (A) Mercury, Venus, Earth, and Mars
   - (B) Venus, Mars, Saturn, and Pluto
   - (C) Jupiter, Saturn, Uranus, and Neptun
   - (D) Jupiter, Saturn, Neptune, and Pluto

7. When a planet's orbit around the sun looks like an oval, it is called _________.
   - (A) An ellipse
   - (B) An eclipse
   - (C) A circle
   - (D) An axis

8. The following planets rotate East to West _________.
   - (A) Earth, Mars
   - (B) Venus, Saturn and Neptune
   - (C) Mercury, Earth and Mars
   - (D) Venus, Uranus

9. Changes in the seasons are caused by _________.

(A) Sunlight and darkness

(B) Rotation of the sun around the earth

(C) Rotation of the sun around the moon

(D) Revolution of the earth around the sun

10. The planet Jupiter has many storms, its most famous is called the ——————.

(A) Great Blue Spot

(B) Big Red

(C) Great Red Spot

(D) Great Green Spot

11. Which two planets cross orbits, sometimes making one closer to the sun than the other?

(A) Mercury and Venus

(B) Jupiter and Saturn

(C) Uranus and Neptune

(D) Neptune and Pluto

12. Which is the largest planet in the solar system?

(A) Venus

(B) Pluto

(C) Earth

(D) Jupiter

13. What makes Uranus look blue-green?

(A) The rocks it is made of

(B) The methane mixed with helium and hydrogen

(C) Its rings

(D) The clouds that surround it

14. Which of the following is true for Orion? Orion is ——————.

(A) The brightest star in the sky

(B) A constellation

(C) The name given to a NASA spacecraft

(D) An asteroid

15. The biggest asteroid known is ——————.

(A) Vesta

(B) Icarus

(C) Ceres

(D) Eros

16. Rounded to the nearest day, the Mercurian year is equal to ——————.

(A) 111 days

(B) 88 days

(C) 50 days

(D) 25 days

17. One Jupiter day is equal to which of the following?

(A) 30 hours 40 mins

(B) 9 hours 50 mins

(C) 3 hours 20 mins

(D) 52 hours 10 mins

18. What is the hottest region of the sun?

(A) The core

(B) The photosphere

(C) The chromosphere

(D) The corona

19. Which civilization developed and implemented the first solar calendar?

(A) Babylonian

(B) Greek

(C) Egyptian

(D) Aztec

20. Name the planet that has the greatest number of known moons ——————.

(A) Earth

(B) Saturn

(C) Jupiter

(D) Mars

21. On which planet can one find the solar system's largest volcano?

(A) Earth

(B) Neptune

(C) Mars

(D) Jupiter

22. Among the sun, moon, and earth, —————— is the biggest and —————— is the smallest heavenly body.

(A) Earth, moon

(B) Sun, moon

(C) Sun, earth

(D) Earth, sun

23. Which of the following is not true in the case of stars?
   (A) They are made up of gases
   (B) They are almost fixed in their places relative to each other
   (C) They are much larger than planets in size
   (D) They twinkle because of irregular emission of light

24. Which one of the following pie-charts represents the fraction of earth that is not covered by water? The shaded part represents the fraction ―――――.

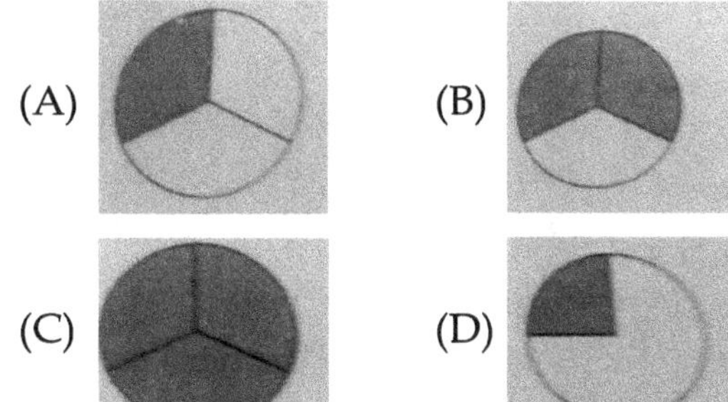

25. Which of the following is not a part of a solar system?
   (A) Earth   (B) Jupiter
   (C) Moon   (D) Pole star

26. The figure below shows the shapes of the moon as seen from the earth on different nights.

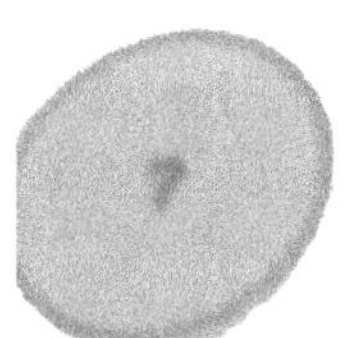  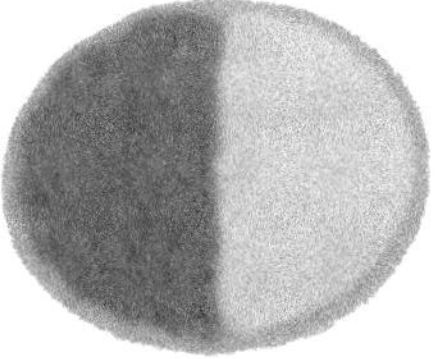 

21 November   **26 November**   **28 November**   **30 November**

Which of the following shows the correct shape of the moon on 28 November?
   (A) Full black   (B) 3/4th moon
   (C) Half moon   (D) Full moon

27. Which is the correct statement regarding the planets?
   (A) The longer the planet takes to revolve around the sun, the higher its temperature.
   (B) The nearer the planet to the sun, the lower its temperature.
   (C) The size of the planet determines its temperature.
   (D) The distance of the planet from the sun determines its temperature.

   (A) Season in the Northern hemisphere can never be the same as the season in the Southern hemisphere.
   (B) Northern hemisphere is away from the sun and the Southern hemisphere is towards it.
   (C) Southern hemisphere is away from the sun and the Northern hemisphere is towards it.
   (D) All of these

28. The axis of the earth is tilted at an angle. This explains why the ―――――.

29. I have 63 moons. I have a big red spot. The spot is a windstorm, swirling around. Which of these planets am I?
   (A) Venus   (B) Jupiter
   (C) Uranus   (D) Saturn

30. What would happen if there was no Jupiter?
   (A) Saturn would be the biggest planet in the solar system.
   (B) Mars would be the coldest planet in the solar system.
   (C) Life would grow on Venus.
   (D) All of these

HOTS (ACHIEVERS SECTION)

31. There are two ecosystems, A and B. Ecosystem A has moist soil, healthy communities, mild temperature, and plenty of water. Ecosystem B has sandy and rocky soil, little or no water, no communities, and very hot temperature.

   I.   Which type of ecosystem is A?
   II. Which type of ecosystem is B?
   III. What is the difference between the types of plants in A and B?

   Now choose the correct option.

	I	II	III
(A)	Forest	Desert	Plants in A will be smaller and fewer than plants in B
(B)	Marsh	Arid	Plants in B will be larger and more abundant
(C)	Forest	Arid	Plants in B will attract more communities
(D)	Forest	Arid	Plants in A will be larger and more in number

32. Two students designed an experiment to study soil erosion. A steady stream of water flows from a faucet into a tray holding sand and gravel. The water forms a channel by eroding some of the sand and gravel. How can the students increase the amount of sand and gravel being eroded?
   (A) By increasing the water temperature.
   (B) By adding coarse gravel to the tray.
   (C) By increasing the tilt of the tray.
   (D) By reducing the amount of flowing water.

33. The picture below shows a place where air currents will form due to the uneven heating of the earth.

   In which direction will the air currents most likely move?

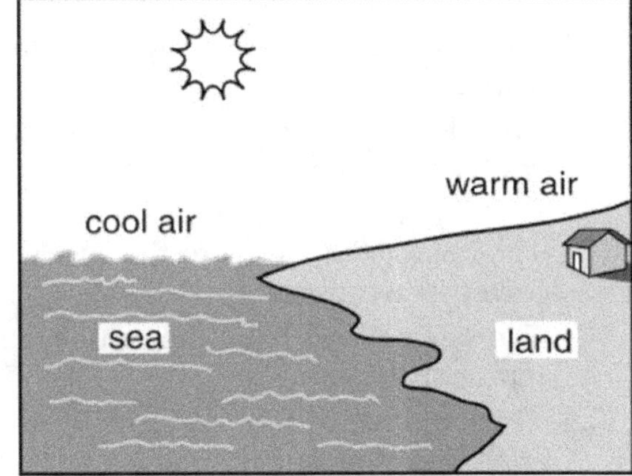

   (A) Straight down over the land.
   (B) From the land towards the sea.
   (C) Straight up above the sea.
   (D) From the sea towards the land.

34. I. The moon maintains its orbit around the earth as a result of?

II. What is the difference between the gravitational force of the Earth and the Moon?

	I	II
(A)	Molecular attraction	The gravitational force of Moon is higher than Earth
(B)	Magnetic attraction	The gravitational force of Moon is equal to that of Earth
(C)	Gravitational attraction	The gravitational force of Earth is higher than that of the Moon
(D)	Solar attraction	The gravitational force of the Moon is lower than that of Earth

35. Pluto was demoted to be a _______ planet in _______.
(A) Dwarf, August 24, 2006
(B) Giant, August 24, 2006
(C) Dwarf, August 15, 2005
(D) Giant, August 15, 2005

1.	Ⓐ Ⓑ Ⓒ Ⓓ	8.	Ⓐ Ⓑ Ⓒ Ⓓ	15.	Ⓐ Ⓑ Ⓒ Ⓓ	22	Ⓐ Ⓑ Ⓒ Ⓓ	29.	Ⓐ Ⓑ Ⓒ Ⓓ
2.	Ⓐ Ⓑ Ⓒ Ⓓ	9.	Ⓐ Ⓑ Ⓒ Ⓓ	16.	Ⓐ Ⓑ Ⓒ Ⓓ	23.	Ⓐ Ⓑ Ⓒ Ⓓ	30.	Ⓐ Ⓑ Ⓒ Ⓓ
3.	Ⓐ Ⓑ Ⓒ Ⓓ	10.	Ⓐ Ⓑ Ⓒ Ⓓ	17.	Ⓐ Ⓑ Ⓒ Ⓓ	24.	Ⓐ Ⓑ Ⓒ Ⓓ	31.	Ⓐ Ⓑ Ⓒ Ⓓ
4.	Ⓐ Ⓑ Ⓒ Ⓓ	11.	Ⓐ Ⓑ Ⓒ Ⓓ	18.	Ⓐ Ⓑ Ⓒ Ⓓ	25.	Ⓐ Ⓑ Ⓒ Ⓓ	32.	Ⓐ Ⓑ Ⓒ Ⓓ
5.	Ⓐ Ⓑ Ⓒ Ⓓ	12.	Ⓐ Ⓑ Ⓒ Ⓓ	19.	Ⓐ Ⓑ Ⓒ Ⓓ	26.	Ⓐ Ⓑ Ⓒ Ⓓ	33.	Ⓐ Ⓑ Ⓒ Ⓓ
6.	Ⓐ Ⓑ Ⓒ Ⓓ	13.	Ⓐ Ⓑ Ⓒ Ⓓ	20.	Ⓐ Ⓑ Ⓒ Ⓓ	27.	Ⓐ Ⓑ Ⓒ Ⓓ	34.	Ⓐ Ⓑ Ⓒ Ⓓ
7.	Ⓐ Ⓑ Ⓒ Ⓓ	14.	Ⓐ Ⓑ Ⓒ Ⓓ	21.	Ⓐ Ⓑ Ⓒ Ⓓ	28.	Ⓐ Ⓑ Ⓒ Ⓓ	35.	Ⓐ Ⓑ Ⓒ Ⓓ

LOGICAL REASONING

LEARNING OBJECTIVES

- ➤ logic of patterns and series
- ➤ identifying the odd one out
- ➤ analogous relation among objects
- ➤ classifying objects as per their common traits
- ➤ rules of coding and decoding
- ➤ arranging words as per dictionary
- ➤ basic knowledge of the dictionary
- ➤ concept of four main directions
- ➤ mirror images
- ➤ water images
- ➤ different shapes
- ➤ 2D and 3D shapes
- ➤ concept of clock and time
- ➤ calculating time in terms of months, weeks and days

MULTIPLE CHOICE QUESTIONS

Directions (1–5): Choose the correct alternative from the given options.

1. Find the odd one out.
   - (A) DE
   - (B) GH
   - (C) LM
   - (D) ON

2. Find the odd one out.
   - (A) BDC
   - (B) EGF
   - (C) HIJ
   - (D) NPO

3. Find the odd one out.
   - (A) RQ
   - (B) NM
   - (C) JI
   - (D) PQ

4. Find the odd one out.
   - (A) XZ
   - (B) VW
   - (C) ST
   - (D) PQ

5. Find the odd one out.
   - (A) ZYX
   - (B) WVU
   - (C) LMC
   - (D) TSR

6. Sword is related to Slaughter in the same way as Scalpel is related to ______.
   - (A) Murder
   - (B) Stab
   - (C) Surgery
   - (D) Chopping

7. Life is related to Autobiography in the same way as Witness is related to ______.
   - (A) Papers
   - (B) Truth
   - (C) Documents
   - (D) Acceptance

8. Chef is related to Restaurant in the same way as Druggist is related to ______.
   - (A) Medicine
   - (B) Pharmacy
   - (C) Store
   - (D) Chemist

9. Jade is related to Green in the same way as Garnet is related to ______.
   - (A) Blue
   - (B) Orange
   - (C) Red
   - (D) Yellow

10. Dancer is related to Stage in the same way as Priest is related to ______.
    - (A) Pulpit
    - (B) Assembly
    - (C) Parliament
    - (D) State

11. Identify the code for RAKESH.
    (A) TCMGOJ
    (B) TCMGUJ
    (C) TCMJUG
    (D) TCMGUT

12. Identify the code for VARSHA.
    (A) XTCUJT
    (B) XCTUJC
    (C) XTCUJC
    (D) CTXUJC

13. Identify the code for THERMAL.
    (A) VJGTOCN
    (B) JVGTOCN
    (C) VJGOTCN
    (D) CTXUJC

14. Identify the code for CHINTU.
    (A) EJKPVW
    (B) EKJPVW
    (C) EKPVWI
    (D) FKLQWX

15. Identify the code PINTU.
    (A) RKPVW
    (B) RKVPW
    (C) PKRVW
    (D) RKPWN

16. Which letter is exactly between R and V?
    (A) S   (B) U
    (C) T   (D) I

17. Which letter is exactly between the English alphabet?
    (A) M   (B) N
    (C) L   (D) No letter

18. Raju is sixth from the left end and Viru is tenth from the right end in a row of boys. If there are eight boys between Raju and Viru, how many boys are there in the row?

    (A) 24   (B) 26
    (C) 23   (D) 25

19. A class of boys stands in a single line, one boy is 19th in order from both the ends. How many boys are there in the class?
    (A) 37   (B) 39
    (C) 27   (D) 38

20. Sameer ranked 9th from the top and 38th from the bottom in a class. How many students are there in the class?
    (A) 45   (B) 47
    (C) 46   (D) 48

21. A river flows west to east and on the way turns left and goes in a semi-circle around a hillock, and then turns left at right angles. In which direction is the river finally flowing?
    (A) West
    (B) East
    (C) North
    (D) South

22. I am facing south. I turn right and walk 20 m. Then I turn right again and walk 10 m. Then I turn left and walk 10 m and then turning right walk 20 m. Then I turn right again and walk 60 m. In which direction am I from the starting point?
    (A) North
    (B) North-west
    (C) East
    (D) North-east

23. A rat runs 20 towards East and turns to right, runs 10 ft and turns to right, runs 9 ft and again turns to left, runs 5 ft and then turns to left, runs 12 ft and finally turns to left and runs 6 ft. Now, in which direction is the rat facing?
    (A) East
    (B) West
    (C) North
    (D) South

24. Starting from a point P, Sachin walked 20 metres towards South. He turned left and walked 30 metres. He then turned left and walked 20 metres. He again turned left and walked 40 metres and reached a point Q. How far and in which direction is the point Q from the point P?
(A) 20 m west
(B) 10 m east
(C) 10 m north
(D) None of these

25. Rohan walks a distance of 3 km towards North, then turns to his left and walks for 2 km. He again turns left and walks for 3 km. At this point he turns to his left and walks for 3 km. How many kilometers is he from the starting point?
(A) 1 km
(B) 2 km
(C) 3 km
(D) 5 km

Direction (26–30): In each of the following questions you are given a combination of letters and/or numbers followed by four alternatives (1), (2), (3) and (4). Choose the alternative which closely resembles the mirror image of the given combination.

26. 247596
(1) 695742
(2) 695742 [mirror]
(3) 695742 [mirror]
(4) 247596 [mirror]
(A) 1
(B) 2
(C) 3
(D) 4

27. BR4AQ16HI
(1) BR4AQ16HI [mirror]
(2) BR4AQ19HI [mirror]
(3) BR4AQ16HI [mirror]
(4) BR4AQ16HI [mirror]
(A) 1
(B) 2
(C) 3
(D) 4

28. GEOGRAPHY
(1) GEOGRAPHY [mirror]
(2) YHPARGOEG
(3) GEOGRAPHY [mirror]
(4) GEOGRAPHY [mirror]
(A) 1
(B) 2
(C) 3
(D) 4

29. NATIONAL
(1) NATIONAL [mirror]
(2) NATIONAL [mirror]
(3) NATIONAL [mirror]
(4) LANOITAN [mirror]
(A) 1
(B) 2
(C) 3
(D) 4

30. PAINTED
(1) PAINTED [mirror]
(2) PAINTED [mirror]
(3) PAINTED [mirror]
(4) PAINTED [mirror]
(A) 1
(B) 2
(C) 3
(D) 4

31. What is the shape with four equal sides?
(A) Rectangle
(B) Square
(C) Triangle
(D) Heptagon

32. Which shape has three sides?
(A) Rectangle
(B) Square
(C) Triangle
(D) Heptagon

33. Which shape has four sides with only two opposite sides equal?
(A) Rectangle
(B) Square
(C) Triangle
(D) Heptagon

34. Which is a 3D shape?
(A) Cube
(B) Square
(C) Triangle
(D) Hexagon

35. Which is a 2D shape?
(A) Cube
(B) Cuboid
(C) Sphere
(D) Heptagon

36. Aditya spent 25 minutes on his home work last night. He started it at 5: 50 pm. What time did he finish his homework?
(A) 5:15
(B) 6:15
(C) 5:10
(D) 6:10

37. The cricket match started at 8:00 pm. Each half was 45 minutes. What time did the first half end?
(A) 8:45pm
(B) 9:30pm
(C) 8:35pm
(D) 9:05pm

38. The school holiday starts in three weeks. School is open 5 days week. How many school days are left until the holiday?
(A) 25 days (B) 21 days
(C) 15 days (D) 20 days

39. It takes 12 minutes to bathe a dog. How long would it take to bathe 10 dogs?

(A) 100 minutes (B) 3hrs.
(C) 60 minutes (D) 120 minutes

40. Maheshwari started her homework at 6:15 pm. How long would it take to do his homework till 7 pm?
(A) 40 minutes (B) 45 min
(C) 50 min (D) 55 min

1.	Ⓐ Ⓑ Ⓒ Ⓓ	9.	Ⓐ Ⓑ Ⓒ Ⓓ	17.	Ⓐ Ⓑ Ⓒ Ⓓ	25	Ⓐ Ⓑ Ⓒ Ⓓ	33.	Ⓐ Ⓑ Ⓒ Ⓓ
2.	Ⓐ Ⓑ Ⓒ Ⓓ	10.	Ⓐ Ⓑ Ⓒ Ⓓ	18.	Ⓐ Ⓑ Ⓒ Ⓓ	26.	Ⓐ Ⓑ Ⓒ Ⓓ	34.	Ⓐ Ⓑ Ⓒ Ⓓ
3.	Ⓐ Ⓑ Ⓒ Ⓓ	11.	Ⓐ Ⓑ Ⓒ Ⓓ	19.	Ⓐ Ⓑ Ⓒ Ⓓ	27.	Ⓐ Ⓑ Ⓒ Ⓓ	35.	Ⓐ Ⓑ Ⓒ Ⓓ
4.	Ⓐ Ⓑ Ⓒ Ⓓ	12.	Ⓐ Ⓑ Ⓒ Ⓓ	20.	Ⓐ Ⓑ Ⓒ Ⓓ	28.	Ⓐ Ⓑ Ⓒ Ⓓ	36.	Ⓐ Ⓑ Ⓒ Ⓓ
5.	Ⓐ Ⓑ Ⓒ Ⓓ	13.	Ⓐ Ⓑ Ⓒ Ⓓ	21.	Ⓐ Ⓑ Ⓒ Ⓓ	29.	Ⓐ Ⓑ Ⓒ Ⓓ	37.	Ⓐ Ⓑ Ⓒ Ⓓ
6.	Ⓐ Ⓑ Ⓒ Ⓓ	14.	Ⓐ Ⓑ Ⓒ Ⓓ	22.	Ⓐ Ⓑ Ⓒ Ⓓ	30.	Ⓐ Ⓑ Ⓒ Ⓓ	38.	Ⓐ Ⓑ Ⓒ Ⓓ
7.	Ⓐ Ⓑ Ⓒ Ⓓ	15.	Ⓐ Ⓑ Ⓒ Ⓓ	23.	Ⓐ Ⓑ Ⓒ Ⓓ	31.	Ⓐ Ⓑ Ⓒ Ⓓ	39.	Ⓐ Ⓑ Ⓒ Ⓓ
8.	Ⓐ Ⓑ Ⓒ Ⓓ	16.	Ⓐ Ⓑ Ⓒ Ⓓ	24.	Ⓐ Ⓑ Ⓒ Ⓓ	32.	Ⓐ Ⓑ Ⓒ Ⓓ	40.	Ⓐ Ⓑ Ⓒ Ⓓ

LOGICAL REASONING

MODEL TEST PAPER

1. See the analogy and choose the correct option.

   Monday: April : : Friday : ?

   (A) July

   (B) Saturday

   (C) August

   (D) Tuesday

2. See the analogy and choose the correct option.

   Disease : Health : : Freedom : ?

   (A) Slavery

   (B) Pleasure

   (C) Plight

   (D) Beauty

3. If LIGHT is coded as GILTH, find the code for RAINY.

   (A) IARYN

   (B) ARINY

   (C) NAIRY

   (D) RINAY

4. In a code language 256 means 'you are good', 637 means 'we are bad', 358 means 'good and bad'. Find the code for 'and'.

   (A) 2   (B) 5

   (C) 8   (D) 3

5. Which of the following diagrams indicates the best relation between Examination, Questions and Practice?

   (A) 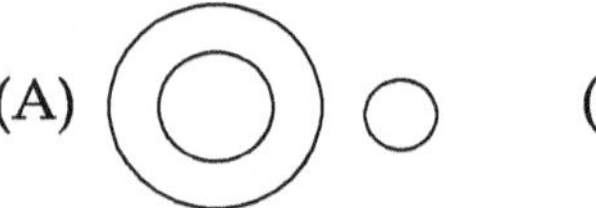   (B) 

   (C) 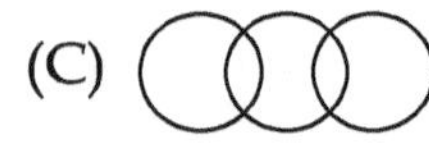   (D) 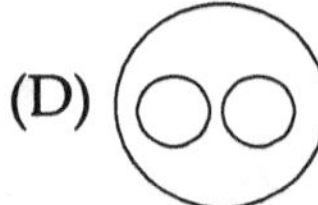

6. The figure shown is of a plant in a beaker. Yesterday, Anaya filled this beaker with water to the top. But today she observed that the level of water has decreased. The reason behind this might be —————.

   (A) Water has disappeared from the beaker.

   (B) Water was absorbed by the roots of the plant.

   (C) Water has frozen.

   (D) Water has condensed.

7. Look at the figure shown below. It is showing the exchange of gases in the leaves at night.

   Which pair of arrows correctly shows the exchange of gases in the leaves at night?

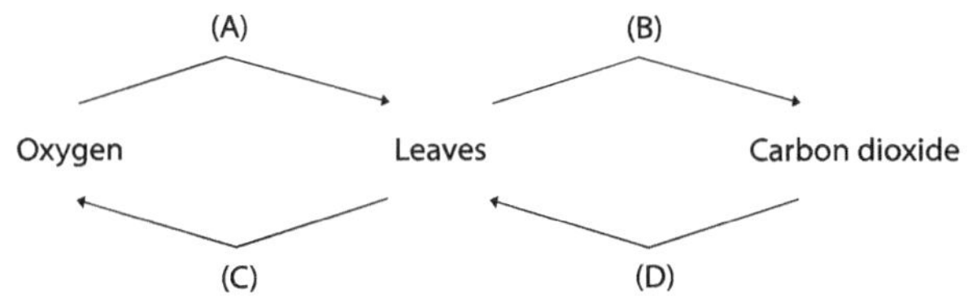

(A) A and B (B) A and C
(C) B and D (D) C and D

8. Which of the following performs photo-synthesis in cactus?
(A) Leaves
(B) Spines
(C) Roots
(D) Stem

9. Which of the following does not need oxygen for respiration?
(A) Mushroom
(B) Parasites
(C) Crabs
(D) Fish

10. Study the following Venn diagram and answer the following question.

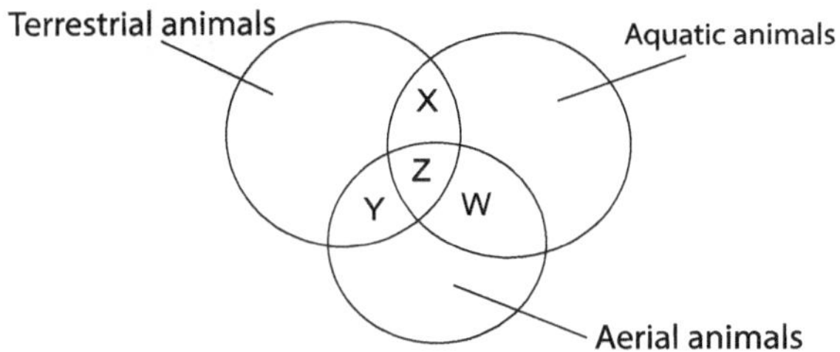

Frogs and salamanders can be placed in which part of the above diagram?
(A) Z (B) Y
(C) X (D) W

11. Water molecules remain in somewhat definite positions with relatively little motion and vibrate back and forth to a limited extent. This would be characteristic of __________.
(A) Water
(B) Steam
(C) Ice
(D) Plasma

12. Oceans have a huge effect on weather and climate mainly because __________.
(A) Oceans have huge waves.
(B) Ocean water is very salty.
(C) The fish and sea creatures give off heat.
(D) Oceans hold and spread heat around the world by water and air currents.

13. What is in the middle of evaporation and precipitation?
(A) Condensation
(B) Evaporation
(C) Run off
(D) Precipitation

14. What blows steadily over long distances in a predictable direction?
(A) Weather
(B) Humidity
(C) Global wind
(D) Insolation

15. A long tube that runs from the mouth to the stomach is called the __________.
(A) Stomach
(B) Liver
(C) Pancreas
(D) Esophagus

16. Three things that bones store inside them are __________.
(A) Lipids, water, calcium
(B) Water, calcium, minerals
(C) Minerals, calcium, lipids

17. We eat more than one part of which plants?
(A) Spinach and lettuce
(B) Beets and onions
(C) Okra and tomatoes
(D) Radish and carrot

18. A section of the earth's crust and mantle that fits together like a puzzle is its _____________.

   (A) Plate   (B) Magma

   (C) Continents   (D) Crust

19. The building blocks of rocks are _________.
   (A) Soil
   (B) Grains
   (C) Minerals
   (D) Sedimentary

20. Gold is the metal that has the highest ductility and malleability. Which is in the second place?
   (A) Silver
   (B) Bronze
   (C) Glass
   (D) Plastic

21. The picture below shows how a pot is made with a lump of clay.

A lump of clay can be moulded to any shape as it has the property of _________.
   (A) Elasticity
   (B) Malleability
   (C) Translucency
   (D) Both (A) and (B)

22. Lexie twists the cap off the bottle of juice. What type of simple machine is the cap?
   (A) Screw
   (B) Pulley
   (C) Wheel and axle
   (D) Inclined plane

23. See the following natural phenomenon and fill in the blanks with from, behind, between.

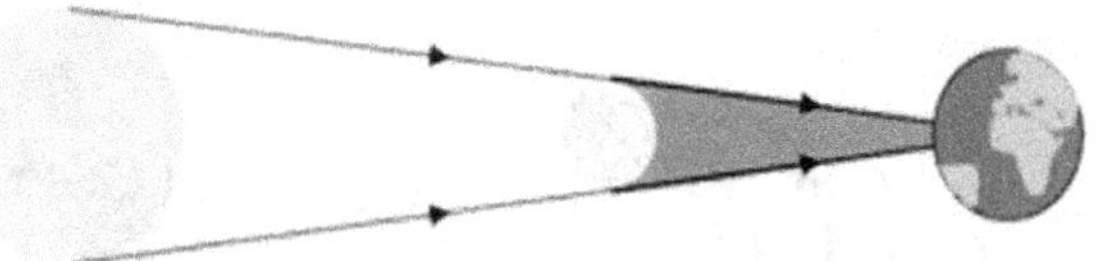

During a solar eclipse, the moon is _____________ the earth and the sun.

_____________ the earth, we see that the sun is _________ the moon.
   (A) Between, from, behind
   (B) Behind, from, between
   (C) From, behind, between
   (D) Between, behind, from

24.

The roofs shown in the above picture _____________.
   (A) Keep the house hot and warm
   (B) Collect snow
   (C) Collect rainwater
   (D) Do not collect snow and rainwater

25. Sanchit stretched a piece of plastic food wrap over a large bowl and secured it firmly in place with a rubber band. He put some green beans on the plastic, then used a spoon to hit the side of the bowl. He saw that the beans bounced all over the plastic producing little tapping noises. Which of the following shows the energy conversions that have taken place?
   (A) Sound → movement
   (B) Only sound

OLYMPIAD WORKBOOK (NSO) CLASS – 4

(C) Only movement

(D) Movement → sound

26. Read the given paragraph.

X and Y are means of transport, which are used for special purposes. X carries fire fighters and their equipment to put out fire, and Y takes sick or injured people to the hospital.

X and Y in the above paragraph are __________.

	X	Y
(A)	Cable car	Aeroplane
(B)	Hot air balloon	Autorickshaw
(C)	Lorry	Truck
(D)	Fire engine	Ambulance

27. Select the incorrect statement from the following.

(A) We must cross the road from wherever we like.

(B) Safety means being careful and avoiding accidents.

(C) There are rules and signs for the safety of people on the roads.

(D) We must use footpaths for walking, and cyclists must always keep to the left.

28. Which of these professionals wear uniforms?

(A) Police

(B) Gatekeeper

(C) Gardener

(D) Both (A) and (B)

29. Look at the following table carefully.

Allow light to pass through	Allow some light to pass through	Do not allow light to pass through
Tracing paper	Glass	Cardboard
Metal can	Clear water	Wood

Which of the following objects is/are incorrectly classified?

(A) Tracing paper and glass

(B) Metal can, clear water, glass, and tracing paper

(C) Wood and glass

(D) Metal can

30. What is formed from trees and other plants that died millions of years ago?

(A) Rocks

(B) Coal

(C) Stones

(D) Marble

31. Study the following diagram and select the correct option.

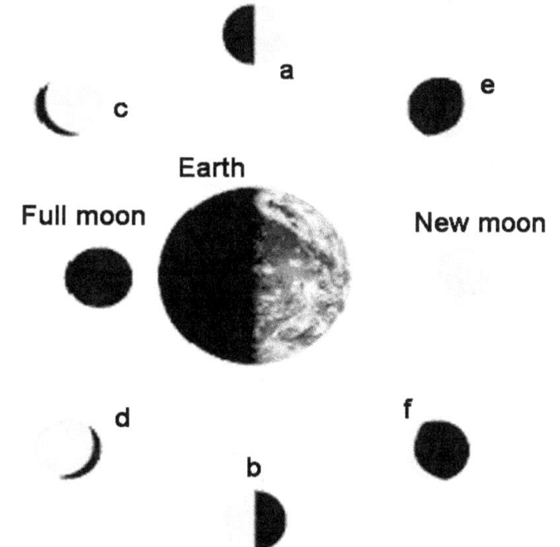

I. Which is the gibbous moon out of a, b, c, d, e, and f?

II. Which is the crescent moon?

III. Which labelling is correct?

	I	II	III
(A)	d and c	e and f	Full moon and new moon
(B)	e and f	d and c	New moon
(C)	a and d	e and f	Full moon
(D)	d and c	e and f	New moon

32. Select the correct match:

	Shape		Function		Teeth
A.	Sharp and flat	1	Chew and grind	W	Molar
B.	Pointed	2	Biting/ cutting	X	Incisors
C.	Broad	3	Tearing	Y	Premolars
D.	Broad	4	Grind	Z	Canines

(A) A-2-W; B-1-X; C-4-Y; D-3-Z
(B) A-3-X; B-4-Z; C-1-W; D-2-Y
(C) A-4-Y; B-2-X; C-3-Z; D-1-W
(D) A-2-X; B-3-Z; C-1-Y; D-4-W

33. The chart below shows temperatures recorded from Monday to Friday during a week in June.

Temperatures for the week

Day	Temperature (°F)	Temperature (°C)
Monday	72	22.2
Tuesday	76	24.4
Wednesday	68	19
Thursday	70	21.1
Friday	70	21.1

I. Which thermometer shows the temperature recorded on Wednesday?

II. In the above table which °F is incorrectly depicted as °C?

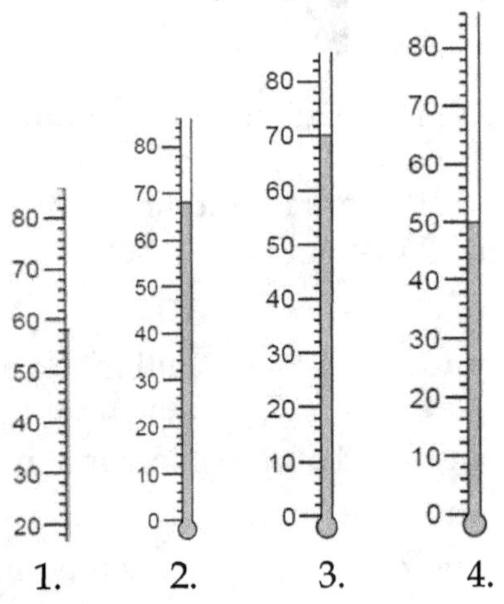

1.   2.   3.   4.

	I	II
(A)	3	76
(B)	2	68
(C)	4	68
(D)	1	72

34.

I. It would be most difficult to ride downhill on this bicycle if __________ were missing.

II. Which simple machine can you locate in a cycle?

	I	II
(A)	The chain	Lever and wheel
(B)	Brakes	Axle and lever
(C)	The kickstand	Lever
(D)	A pedal	Wheel and axle and lever

35. The amount of direct sunlight the Northern Hemisphere receives changes throughout the year. The diagram below shows Earth revolving around the Sun.

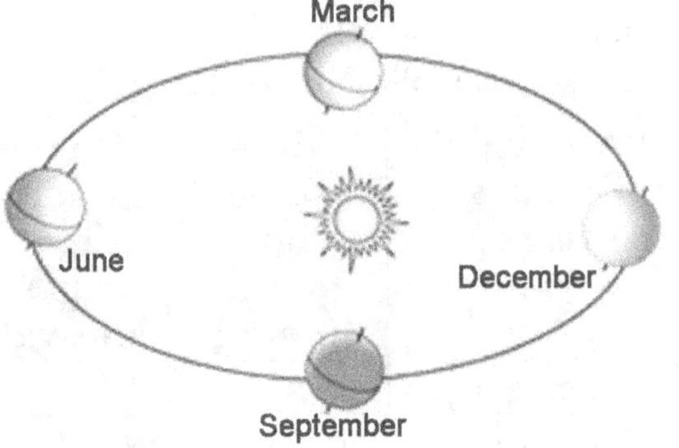

OLYMPIAD WORKBOOK (NSO) CLASS—4

I. In which month will the Northern Hemisphere receive the greatest amount of direct sunlight?

II. In which month will the Spring season begin in the Northern Hemisphere?

	I	II
(A)	March	June
(B)	June	March
(C)	September	January
(D)	December	March

1.	Ⓐ Ⓑ Ⓒ Ⓓ	8.	Ⓐ Ⓑ Ⓒ Ⓓ	15.	Ⓐ Ⓑ Ⓒ Ⓓ	22	Ⓐ Ⓑ Ⓒ Ⓓ	29.	Ⓐ Ⓑ Ⓒ Ⓓ
2.	Ⓐ Ⓑ Ⓒ Ⓓ	9.	Ⓐ Ⓑ Ⓒ Ⓓ	16.	Ⓐ Ⓑ Ⓒ Ⓓ	23.	Ⓐ Ⓑ Ⓒ Ⓓ	30.	Ⓐ Ⓑ Ⓒ Ⓓ
3.	Ⓐ Ⓑ Ⓒ Ⓓ	10.	Ⓐ Ⓑ Ⓒ Ⓓ	17.	Ⓐ Ⓑ Ⓒ Ⓓ	24.	Ⓐ Ⓑ Ⓒ Ⓓ	31.	Ⓐ Ⓑ Ⓒ Ⓓ
4.	Ⓐ Ⓑ Ⓒ Ⓓ	11.	Ⓐ Ⓑ Ⓒ Ⓓ	18.	Ⓐ Ⓑ Ⓒ Ⓓ	25.	Ⓐ Ⓑ Ⓒ Ⓓ	32.	Ⓐ Ⓑ Ⓒ Ⓓ
5.	Ⓐ Ⓑ Ⓒ Ⓓ	12.	Ⓐ Ⓑ Ⓒ Ⓓ	19.	Ⓐ Ⓑ Ⓒ Ⓓ	26.	Ⓐ Ⓑ Ⓒ Ⓓ	33.	Ⓐ Ⓑ Ⓒ Ⓓ
6.	Ⓐ Ⓑ Ⓒ Ⓓ	13.	Ⓐ Ⓑ Ⓒ Ⓓ	20.	Ⓐ Ⓑ Ⓒ Ⓓ	27.	Ⓐ Ⓑ Ⓒ Ⓓ	34.	Ⓐ Ⓑ Ⓒ Ⓓ
7.	Ⓐ Ⓑ Ⓒ Ⓓ	14.	Ⓐ Ⓑ Ⓒ Ⓓ	21.	Ⓐ Ⓑ Ⓒ Ⓓ	28.	Ⓐ Ⓑ Ⓒ Ⓓ	35.	Ⓐ Ⓑ Ⓒ Ⓓ

HINTS AND SOLUTIONS

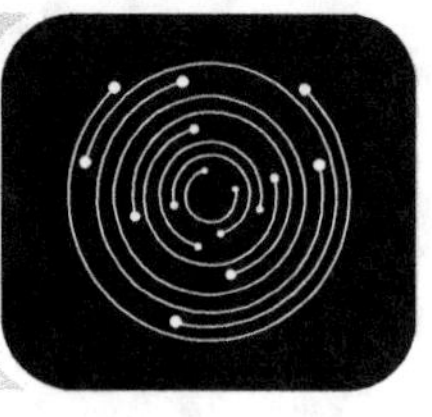

1. PLANT LIFE

Answer Key

1. (C)	2. (C)	3. (A)	4. (D)	5. (C)	6. (D)	7. (B)	8. (B)	9. (D)	10. (B)
11. (A)	12. (D)	13. (A)	14. (C)	15. (B)	16. (D)	17. (D)	18. (C)	19. (C)	20. (B)
21. (C)	22. (B)	23. (C)	24. (B)	25. (B)	26. (B)	27. (C)	28. (B)	29. (B)	30. (C)

HOTS (ACHIEVERS SECTION)

31. (B)	32. (A)	33. (C)	34. (D)	35. (D)

33. (C)

The given experiment demonstrates that oxygen is evolved during the process of photosynthesis. In this experiment, the aquatic plant-like Hydrilla is used. The aspect is the light reaction of photosynthesis. This is the process in which the plants with the help of chloroplast captures light energy. They can use the carbon dioxide from the air to produce carbohydrates in the form of sugar and starch. There is a splitting of water to fill the gap created by the electron in the photosystem. The product which is formed is oxygen which is liberated during this process. Since, test tube B does not contain hydrilla in it, it will not form any gas.

35. (D)

Plants need water, sunlight and chlorophyll to synthesize food.

2. ANIMAL LIFE

Answer Key

1. (B)	2. (D)	3. (D)	4. (C)	5. (D)	6. (D)	7. (A)	8. (B)	9. (B)	10. (C)
11. (B)	12. (B)	13. (A)	14. (C)	15. (B)	16. (A)	17. (A)	18. (D)	19. (B)	20. (A)
21. (C)	22. (B)	23. (A)	24. (B)	25. (A)	26. (B)	27. (D)	28. (B)	29. (C)	30. (C)

HOTS (ACHIEVERS SECTION)

1. (A)	2. (D)	3. (A)	4. (C)	5. (D)

3. HUMAN BODY

Answer Key

1. (D)	2. (B)	3. (A)	4. (C)	5. (D)	6. (B)	7. (C)	8. (A)	9. (B)	10. (C)
11. (A)	12. (C)	13. (A)	14. (D)	15. (C)	16. (A)	17. (D)	18. (D)	19. (A)	20. (C)
21. (A)	22. (C)	23. (D)	24. (D)	25. (A)	26. (B)	27. (C)	28. (C)	29. (C)	30. (B)

HOTS (ACHIEVERS SECTION)

31. (D)	32. (A)	33. (A)	34. (C)	35. (D)

33. (A)

Running will increase our heart rate as it requires more energy from our body which needs quick pumping of blood from the heart.

34. (C)

The innermost layer or lining (mucosa) contains the glands that release digestive juices. This is the first and innermost layer or lining. It contains the glands that release digestive juices. These are called hydrochloric acid and pepsin.

4. FOOD, HEALTH AND SANITATION

Answer Key

1. (B)	2. (C)	3. (D)	4. (A)	5. (B)	6. (B)	7. (A)	8. (B)	9. (B)	10. (A)
11. (C)	12. (D)	13. (C)	14. (B)	15. (B)	16. (A)	17. (D)	18. (C)	19. (C)	20. (C)
21. (C)	22. (D)	23. (B)	24. (C)	25. (C)	26. (A)	27. (D)	28. (A)	29. (B)	30. (C)

HOTS (ACHIEVERS SECTION)

1. (D)	2. (A)	3. (C)	4. (B)	5. (D)

5. HUMAN NEEDS

Answer Key

1. (D)	2. (D)	3. (B)	4. (C)	5. (B)	6. (C)	7. (A)	8. (C)	9. (C), (D)	10. (D)
11. (B)	12. (A)	13. (B)	14. (B)	15. (B)	16. (A)	17. (B)	18. (C)	19. (B)	20. (C)
21. (D)	22. (B)	23. (A)	24. (C)	25. (C)					

HOTS (ACHIEVERS SECTION)

26. (D)	27. (C)	28. (C)	29. (B)	30. (B)

6. MATTER AND MATERIALS

Answer Key

1. (A)	2. (D)	3. (A)	4. (D)	5. (C)	6. (C)	7. (A)	8. (D)	9. (C)	10. (D)
11. (D)	12. (D)	13. (C)	14. (B)	15. (A)	16. (D)	17. (A)	18. (D)	19. (A)	20. (B)
21. (C)	22. (C)	23. (B)	24. (B)	25. (A)					

HOTS (ACHIEVERS SECTION)

1. (C)	2. (C)	3. (A)	4. (B)	5. (A)

7. WORK, FORCE AND ENERGY

Answer Key

1. (C)	2. (B)	3. (B)	4. (C)	5. (A)	6. (C)	7. (D)	8. (B)	9. (D)	10. (A)
11. (B)	12. (B)	13. (C)	14. (D)	15. (A)	16. (D)	17. (C)	18. (A)	19. (D)	20. (D)
21. (D)	22. (B)	23. (B)	24. (B)	25. (B)	26. (B)	27. (D)	28. (D)	29. (A)	30. (C)

HOTS (ACHIEVERS SECTION)

1. (B)	2. (C)	3. (A)	4. (C)	5. (C)

8. OUR ENVIRONMENT

Answer Key

1. (C)	2. (C)	3. (A)	4. (B)	5. (C)	6. (B)	7. (C)	8. (B)	9. (B)	10. (C)
11. (D)	12. (B)	13. (D)	14. (D)	15. (C)	16. (B)	17. (B)	18. (A)	19. (B)	20. (D)

1. **(C)**
Sewage is a liquid waste which has water as its largest component along with various types of impurities like wastewater from houses is called sewage.

2. **(C)**
Global Warming is the gradual increase in the overall temperature of the Earth's atmosphere. It begins with a phenomenon called the greenhouse effect.

3. **(A)**
The outermost layer, called the crust, is solid, too. Together, these solid parts are called the lithosphere. Earth's crust is made up of hard rocks. It is the only part of the Earth that humans see.

4. **(B)**
Cutting down trees on a large scale is called deforestation, which is done majorly for commercial purposes such as to start big industries by clearing the land.

5. **(C)**
In this case burning, burying and

dumping will not work, as burning will cause air pollution, burying and dumping will cause land pollution. Recycling is an option which best to prevent pollution or causing any harm to environment.

6. **(B)**

A large fraction of the emitted ODSs reach the stratosphere, where they are converted to reactive gases containing chlorine and bromine that lead to ozone depletion. ODSs containing only carbon, chlorine, and fluorine are called chlorofluorocarbons, usually abbreviated as CFCs.

7. **(C)**

The plant helps to provide oxygen for animal respiration. they also maintain the balance of carbon-di-oxide in the atmosphere. that is why forest is called 'lungs of nature'.

8. **(B)**

The mass of air surrounding the earth is known as atmosphere.

9. **(B)**

Contamination unwanted substances into water is called water pollution.

10. **(C)**

Earth—our home planet—is the only place we know of so far that's inhabited by living things. It's also the only planet in our solar system with liquid water on the surface.

11. **(D)**

Living things like plants and animals are called biotic components. Non-living things like air, light, water, soil, and temperature are called abiotic components. Out of all these, plants cover the most of the Earth.

12. **(B)**

Generally speaking, South Indian cooking is based around rice, lentils, and stews. Dishes such as dosa (a lentil and rice crêpe), idli (steamed lentil rice cakes), saaru/rasam (tomato, tamarind, and lentil soup), and huli/sambar (spicy lentil and vegetable stew) are all from the South.

13. **(D)**

Acid rain leaches aluminium from the soil. That aluminium may be harmful to plants as well as animals. Acid rain also removes minerals and nutrients from the soil that trees need to grow. The trees are then less able to absorb sunlight, which makes them weak and less able to withstand freezing temperatures.

14. **(D)**

Mahl and Portuguese are minority languages.

15. **(C)**

Biodegradable materials are those, which degrade or break down in a natural manner. ... For instance, fruits, vegetables, flowers, plants, animals, water, paper and more are examples of biodegradable waste. They transform into simpler units and then we use them as fertilizers, manure, compost, biogas and more.

16. **(B)**

Habitat destruction is currently considered the primary cause of species extinction worldwide. Environmental factors can contribute to habitat destruction more indirectly. Geological processes, climate change, introduction of invasive species, ecosystem nutrient depletion, water and noise pollution are some examples.

17. **(B)**

Humans need to interact with the environment to obtain our food, water, fuel, medicines, building materials and many other things. Advances in science and technology have helped us to exploit the environment for our benefit, but we have also introduced pollution and caused environmental damage.

18. (A)

Independence Day, Republic Day and Gandhi Jayanti are national festivals of India.

19. (A)

Hindi in Devanagari script is the official language of the Union. The form of numerals to be used for official purposes of the Union is the international form of Indian numerals {Article 343 (1) of the Constitution}. In addition to Hindi language.English language may also be used for official purposes.

20. (D)

Rajasthani, Bihari, Haryanavi are regional languages.

HOTS (ACHIEVERS SECTION)

21. (D)	22. (A)	23. (C)	24. (C)	25. (C)

9. EARTH AND UNIVERSE

Answer Key

1. (A)	2. (D)	3. (B)	4. (B)	5. (C)	6. (C)	7. (A)	8. (D)	9. (D)	10. (C)
11. (D)	12. (D)	13. (B)	14. (B)	15. (C)	16. (B)	17. (B)	18. (D)	19. (C)	20. (B)
21. (C)	22. (B)	23. (B)	24. (D)	25. (D)	26. (C)	27. (D)	28. (A)	29. (B)	30. (A)

HOTS (ACHIEVERS SECTION)

31. (D)	32. (C)	33. (D)	34. (C)	35. (A)

10. LOGICAL REASONING

Answer Key

1. (D)	2. (C)	3. (D)	4. (A)	5. (C)	6. (C)	7. (C)	8. (B)	9. (C)	10. (A)
11. (B)	12. (B)	13. (A)	14. (A)	15. (A)	16. (C)	17. (D)	18. (A)	19. (A)	20. (C)
21. (B)	22. (D)	23. (C)	24. (C)	25. (A)	26. (D)	27. (A)	28. (A)	29. (B)	30. (B)
31. (B)	32. (C)	33. (A)	34. (A)	35. (D)	36. (B)	37. (A)	38. (C)	39. (D)	40. (B)

1. (D)

   $D + 1 = E, G + 1 = H, L + 1 = M$
   but, $O - 1 = N$

3. (D)

   $R - 1 = Q, N - 1 = M, J - 1 = I$
   but, $P + 1 = Q$

4. (A)

   $V + 1 = W, S + 1 = T, P + 1 = Q$
   but, $X + 2 = Z$

5. (C)

   Pattern is reverse writing of letters.
   $Z \leftarrow Y \leftarrow X$; $W \leftarrow V \leftarrow U$; $T \leftarrow S \leftarrow R$, but it is
   not so in case of LMN.

6. (C)

   Second denotes the purpose for which the first is used.

7. (C)

   Second contains an account of the first.

8. (B)

   Second is the working place of the first.

9. (C)

   Jade is a green precious stone and garnet is a red precious stone.

10. (A)

    Second is the place for the first to perform on.

16. (C)

    R S T U V

    T is exactly between R and V.

17. (D)

    There are 26 letters in the English alphabet. M and N are the two letters in between, but no single letter exists between M and N.

MODEL TEST PAPER

Answer Key

1. (C)	2. (A)	3. (A)	4. (C)	5. (C)	6. (B)	7. (A)	8. (D)	9. (B)	10. (C)
11. (C)	12. (D)	13. (A)	14. (C)	15. (D)	16. (C)	17. (D)	18. (A)	19. (C)	20. (A)
21. (B)	22. (A)	23. (A)	24. (D)	25. (D)	26. (D)	27. (A)	28. (D)	29. (B)	30. (B)
31. (A)	32. (D)	33. (B)	34. (B)	35. (B)					

SAMPLE OMR ANSWER SHEET

1. STUDENT NAME (IN ENGLISH CAPITAL LETTERS ONLY)

Students must write and darken the respective circles completely using HB Pencil only. Othewise their Answer Sheets will not be evaluated.

PERSONAL DETAILS

2. SCHOOL CODE

3. CLASS

4. SECTION

5. ROLL NO.

6. QUESTION PAPER SET

A ○
B ○
C ○
D ○

7. MOBILE NUMBER

8. GENDER

MALE ○
FEMALE ○

9. STREAM
(Only for Class XI and XII Students)

MATHEMATICS ○
BIOLOGY ○
OTHERS ○

MARK YOUR ANSWERS

	A	B	C	D			A	B	C	D
1.	Ⓐ	Ⓑ	Ⓒ	Ⓓ	26.	Ⓐ	Ⓑ	Ⓒ	Ⓓ
2.	Ⓐ	Ⓑ	Ⓒ	Ⓓ	27.	Ⓐ	Ⓑ	Ⓒ	Ⓓ
3.	Ⓐ	Ⓑ	Ⓒ	Ⓓ	28.	Ⓐ	Ⓑ	Ⓒ	Ⓓ
4.	Ⓐ	Ⓑ	Ⓒ	Ⓓ	29.	Ⓐ	Ⓑ	Ⓒ	Ⓓ
5.	Ⓐ	Ⓑ	Ⓒ	Ⓓ	30.	Ⓐ	Ⓑ	Ⓒ	Ⓓ
6.	Ⓐ	Ⓑ	Ⓒ	Ⓓ	31.	Ⓐ	Ⓑ	Ⓒ	Ⓓ
7.	Ⓐ	Ⓑ	Ⓒ	Ⓓ	32.	Ⓐ	Ⓑ	Ⓒ	Ⓓ
8.	Ⓐ	Ⓑ	Ⓒ	Ⓓ	33.	Ⓐ	Ⓑ	Ⓒ	Ⓓ
9.	Ⓐ	Ⓑ	Ⓒ	Ⓓ	34.	Ⓐ	Ⓑ	Ⓒ	Ⓓ
10.	Ⓐ	Ⓑ	Ⓒ	Ⓓ	35.	Ⓐ	Ⓑ	Ⓒ	Ⓓ
11.	Ⓐ	Ⓑ	Ⓒ	Ⓓ	36.	Ⓐ	Ⓑ	Ⓒ	Ⓓ
12.	Ⓐ	Ⓑ	Ⓒ	Ⓓ	37.	Ⓐ	Ⓑ	Ⓒ	Ⓓ
13.	Ⓐ	Ⓑ	Ⓒ	Ⓓ	38.	Ⓐ	Ⓑ	Ⓒ	Ⓓ
14.	Ⓐ	Ⓑ	Ⓒ	Ⓓ	39.	Ⓐ	Ⓑ	Ⓒ	Ⓓ
15.	Ⓐ	Ⓑ	Ⓒ	Ⓓ	40.	Ⓐ	Ⓑ	Ⓒ	Ⓓ
16.	Ⓐ	Ⓑ	Ⓒ	Ⓓ	41.	Ⓐ	Ⓑ	Ⓒ	Ⓓ
17.	Ⓐ	Ⓑ	Ⓒ	Ⓓ	42.	Ⓐ	Ⓑ	Ⓒ	Ⓓ
18.	Ⓐ	Ⓑ	Ⓒ	Ⓓ	43.	Ⓐ	Ⓑ	Ⓒ	Ⓓ
19.	Ⓐ	Ⓑ	Ⓒ	Ⓓ	44.	Ⓐ	Ⓑ	Ⓒ	Ⓓ
20.	Ⓐ	Ⓑ	Ⓒ	Ⓓ	45.	Ⓐ	Ⓑ	Ⓒ	Ⓓ
21.	Ⓐ	Ⓑ	Ⓒ	Ⓓ	46.	Ⓐ	Ⓑ	Ⓒ	Ⓓ
22.	Ⓐ	Ⓑ	Ⓒ	Ⓓ	47.	Ⓐ	Ⓑ	Ⓒ	Ⓓ
23.	Ⓐ	Ⓑ	Ⓒ	Ⓓ	48.	Ⓐ	Ⓑ	Ⓒ	Ⓓ
24.	Ⓐ	Ⓑ	Ⓒ	Ⓓ	49.	Ⓐ	Ⓑ	Ⓒ	Ⓓ
25.	Ⓐ	Ⓑ	Ⓒ	Ⓓ	50.	Ⓐ	Ⓑ	Ⓒ	Ⓓ

Signature of the Student & Date of Examination

Signature of the Invigilator & Date of Examination

V&S Publishers, F-2/16 Ansari Road, Daryaganj, New Delhi-110002, ☎ 011-23240026-27
✉ info@vspublishers.com, 🌐 www.vspublishers.com